David Masson, John Bruce

The Quarrel Between the Earl of Manchester and Oliver Cromwell

An episode of the English Civil War

David Masson, John Bruce

The Quarrel Between the Earl of Manchester and Oliver Cromwell
An episode of the English Civil War

ISBN/EAN: 9783337402877

Printed in Europe, USA, Canada, Australia, Japan

Cover: Foto ©ninafisch / pixelio.de

More available books at **www.hansebooks.com**

THE QUARREL

BETWEEN

THE EARL OF MANCHESTER

AND

OLIVER CROMWELL:

AN EPISODE OF THE ENGLISH CIVIL WAR.

UNPUBLISHED DOCUMENTS RELATING THERETO,
COLLECTED BY THE LATE JOHN BRUCE, F.S.A., &c.;

WITH FRAGMENTS OF

A HISTORICAL PREFACE BY MR. BRUCE,

ANNOTATED AND COMPLETED BY DAVID MASSON.

PRINTED FOR THE CAMDEN SOCIETY.

M.DCCC.LXXV.

WESTMINSTER :
PRINTED BY NICHOLS AND SONS,
25, PARLIAMENT STREET.

[NEW SERIES XII.]

COUNCIL OF THE CAMDEN SOCIETY
FOR THE YEAR 1874-75.

President.

THE RIGHT HON. THE EARL OF VERULAM, F.R.G.S.

WILLIAM CHAPPELL, ESQ. F.S.A., *Treasurer.*
WILLIAM DURRANT COOPER, ESQ. F.S.A.
HENRY CHARLES COOTE, ESQ. F.S.A.
FREDERICK WILLIAM COSENS, ESQ.
JAMES GAIRDNER, ESQ.
SAMUEL RAWSON GARDINER, ESQ., *Director.*
ALFRED KINGSTON, ESQ., *Secretary.*
SIR JOHN MACLEAN, F.S.A.
FREDERIC OUVRY, ESQ. V.P. S.A.
JAMES ORCHARD PHILLIPPS, ESQ. F.R.S. F.S.A.
EDWARD RIMBAULT, LL.D.
REV. W. SPARROW SIMPSON, D.D. F.S.A.
JAMES SPEDDING, ESQ.
WILLIAM JOHN THOMS, ESQ. F.S.A.
J. R. DANIEL-TYSSEN, ESQ.

The COUNCIL of the CAMDEN SOCIETY desire it to be understood that they are not answerable for any opinions or observations that may appear in the Society's publications; the Editors of the several Works being alone responsible for the same.

INTRODUCTORY NOTE.

At the death of Mr. Bruce, in October 1869, there was found among his papers a quantity of manuscript relating to the quarrel between the Earl of Manchester and Cromwell in the year 1644, and showing that he had been minutely studying that incident in the History of the English Civil War, and meant to make it the subject of some publication. The MSS. consisted of (1) Copies of previously unpublished documents recovered by Mr. Bruce's research; (2) Fragments of a Historical Preface, in which Mr. Bruce meant to tell the whole story at some considerable length, by weaving the information from these documents into that otherwise accessible; and (3) Miscellaneous jottings towards the completion of this Preface, chiefly in the form of extracts from the Lords and Commons Journals, but with notes of dates and stray facts besides.

The documentary matter, as left by Mr. Bruce, and as put to press by the Council of the Camden Society for this volume, is partly from the Public Record Office, partly from the Manchester Family Papers at Kimbolton. From the Letter-Books of the Derby House Committee or Committee of Both Kingdoms, preserved in the Record Office, are the copies of the correspondence between that Committee and the Earl of Manchester from July to November 1644, occupying pp. 1–58 of the present volume; and from the Domestic State Papers in the Record Office is the document entitled *Cromwell's Narrative* (pp. 78–95). The remaining three documents, entitled *Narrative of the Earl of Manchester's Campaign* (pp. 59–70), *Statement by an Opponent of Cromwell* (pp. 71–77), and *Notes of Evidence*, &c. (pp. 96–99), are from the Kimbolton Papers. The footnotes to the documents are by Mr. Bruce, except those signed " G. C.," which are by Colonel Colomb.

The Council of the Camden Society having sent me the documents in their present printed form, together with the MS. fragments of Mr. Bruce's intended Historical Preface and the miscellaneous

MS. jottings he had left besides, I have had much pleasure, both from respect to Mr. Bruce's memory and from interest in the subject, in complying with their request that I would do what might be necessary or possible towards completing the Preface. The result has been as follows:—Every word of Mr. Bruce's Preface, so far as it had been written, has been religiously kept; and the completion has been endeavoured in the three forms of *Notes*, *Insertions*, and *Continuation*. The *Notes* (initialed where they are not Mr. Bruce's own) are few. The *Insertions*, always given within brackets, are either attempts to fill up gaps left in Mr. Bruce's manuscript, and which he meant to fill up at his leisure, or they are additions necessary for the coherence of the story at points where I could perceive that Mr. Bruce would almost certainly have made some such additions in revising what he had written. The *Continuation* was a more troublesome affair. Mr. Bruce had, unfortunately, broken off just as he was approaching the heart of his subject, and when he had begun a more minute style of narrative in preparation for what was coming. To have huddled up the sequel in a mere casual paragraph or two would have been to leave Mr. Bruce's design unintelligible. It would have done no manner of justice either to the documents he had collected or to the perception that had actuated him in collecting them and in writing his Preface so far—the perception, namely, of the significance of the quarrel between Manchester and Cromwell, and its involution with all that was most important in a whole important year of English history. I tried, therefore, to put myself in Mr. Bruce's place, and to finish his Preface on his own plan, by combining the material supplied by the documents with that to be found in Rushworth, Baillie, the Journals of the Lords and Commons, and other standard authorities. The extracts he had himself made from the Journals, with such hints as I could gather from his other MS. jottings, have been of use both in the *Continuation* and in the *Insertions*; and I have thought it right carefully to note every instance of help thus received from his own dead hand.

DAVID MASSON.

Edinburgh: February 1875.

CONTENTS.

	PAGE
HISTORICAL PREFACE	v
DOCUMENTS:—	
I. CORRESPONDENCE BETWEEN THE EARL OF MANCHESTER AND THE COMMITTEE OF BOTH KINGDOMS	1
II. NARRATIVE OF THE EARL OF MANCHESTER'S CAMPAIGN	59
III. STATEMENT BY AN OPPONENT OF CROMWELL	71
IV. CROMWELL'S NARRATIVE	78
V. NOTES OF EVIDENCE AGAINST THE EARL OF MANCHESTER	96

HISTORICAL PREFACE.

It is a mere truism in the history of revolutions to assert that they are seldom brought to a close by the persons or political parties with whom they originate. Men whose existence was perhaps scarcely known to the world at large when the onward movement took its origin rise in succession to the surface, acquire the government, and carry forward the work to lengths and heights which their predecessors never contemplated. It is in tracing this sequence of political parties, the gradual growth of what was looked upon in the first instance as a contemptible and almost senseless faction, its struggles for the mastery, the arts (too often unworthy) by which it acquired the ascendancy, its acts whilst in a condition of dominancy, and finally the errors by which it forfeited power and made way for the next in turn, that much of the interest of historical narrative is found.

It is to an incident in a movement of this nature which took place in the course of our great national revolution in the reign of Charles I. that I have now to direct attention.

The Quarrel between Oliver Cromwell and the Earl of Manchester, at the close of the campaign of 1644, is a great leading incident in the history of our Civil War. It brought to the surface and into direct antagonism principles of the very deepest significance in reference to the management of the war, and the triumph of the movement party on that occasion led directly to the ruin of the royal cause.

Our information respecting this important incident is singularly incomplete. Brief entries which refer to it occur on the Journals of the two Houses of Parliament; some papers and notes of speeches relating to it are published in Rushworth and Nalson; and Clarendon and the memoir-writers have told us with more or less inaccuracy what they could recollect, mostly after the lapse of many years.[a] From such weak and incomplete authorities historical writers have inferred the particulars of what occurred, and the degree in which their statements are mere guesswork may be gathered from the fact that in none of the authorities to which we have alluded is there any definite statement of the facts which Cromwell alleged in the House of Commons against the Earl of Manchester in the way of charge, nor of those which the Earl adduced against Cromwell in the House of Lords in the way of answer and recrimination.[b]

In the course of the operations which are in progress among the State Papers under the direction of the Master of the Rolls, some documents have lately been found which establish upon the most certain of all authorities, that of Cromwell himself, what were the assertions on one side of this momentous controversy. These are the papers to which attention is now solicited; but in order to make their meaning and importance palpable we must preface them with some notice of the events out of which they arose.

The Earl of Manchester, whose conduct forms the special point of this inquiry [*i.e.* Edward Montagu, second Earl of Manchester], is principally known in our history by the circumstance that, when

[a] Mr. Bruce's references here are to Rushworth, v. 732-736; Clarendon, 514 *et seq.* (ed. 1843); and, perhaps, under the name of "Memoir-writers," to Baillie, ii. 229-30, 234-5, 244-7; Whitlocke, i. 343 *et seq.* (ed. 1853); Walker's *History of Independency*, part i.; and Holles's *Memoirs*, 18-28. Baillie's jottings on the subject are, however, strictly contemporary.—D.M.

[b] Among modern accounts of the quarrel between Cromwell and Manchester are Godwin's in his *History of the Commonwealth* (i. 378-413) and Mr. Carlyle's in his *Letters and Speeches of Cromwell* (i. 146-150, and 159-163, ed. 1857). Godwin does found only on the authorities mentioned by Mr. Bruce; but Mr. Carlyle had before him other documents, communicated to him by the Duke of Manchester from the family papers at Kimbolton, including that printed in the present volume under the title "Narrative of the Earl of Manchester's Campaign."—D.M.

Lord Kimbolton, by which title he was called up to the House of Peers during the lifetime of his father, he was joined in the charge of high-treason with Pym, Hampden, Strode, Holles, and Haselrig, whom Charles I. went to the House of Commons to arrest. This circumstance, and the conjunction in which Clarendon places him with the Earl of Bedford and Lord Saye, as the three "great contrivers and designers" in the House of Peers,[a] sufficiently mark his political opinions. Dedications to him of religious books by clergymen of the school then termed puritanical indicate that he belonged to that large class of persons who, under the influence of dissatisfaction with the conduct of the bishops and the state of the Church and the clergy, thought it necessary for the preservation of Protestantism that there should be large alterations in the framework of the established Church. In his individual character, every one attests that he was one of the most amiable and most liberal of men. If Clarendon is to be believed, he was indeed too liberal by far. He did not wait to play the part of the lavish heir with the estate which his father had accumulated, by means which "exposed him to some inconvenience and many reproaches,"[b] but during his father's lifetime, for the mere advantage of his party, as Clarendon assures us, he lived far beyond "the narrow exhibition allowed him by his wary father," and thus involved himself in "a great debt,"[c] which drove him into seclusion for many years. Still, whether in the country or at the Court, the Royalist historian is obliged to admit that, " by his natural civility, good manners, and good nature, which flowed towards all men, he was universally acceptable and beloved."[d]

[From several loose sheets containing notes and references in Mr. Bruce's hand, and in that of a correspondent of his, it seems as if he had intended to involve in this Preface, or to append to it, a somewhat detailed memoir of the Earl of Man-

[a] Clarendon, *Hist. Rebell.* p. 73, ed. 1843.
[b] Ibid. p. 22.   [c] Ibid. p. 73.
[d] Ibid. p. 74.

chester. The following may here suffice for that part of the Earl's life which precedes the point at which Mr. Bruce's narrative begins:—He was born in 1602, the eldest son of the lawyer Sir Henry Montagu, who, after various intermediate promotions, became in 1625-26 the first Earl of Manchester, and continued to be one of the councillors and ministers of Charles I. He was educated at Sidney Sussex College, Cambridge, which he entered in January 1617-18, just after Cromwell, who was three years his senior, had left the same college. Having returned to Court, he attended Prince Charles to Spain; and the intimacy thus established between him and Charles lasted for some time after Charles came to the throne. After having sat in the Commons as knight for Huntingdonshire in Charles's first and second Parliaments, he was raised to the Upper House in 1626 by the title of Baron Montagu of Kimbolton; and for the next sixteen years some confusion is caused by the fact that he is heard of both by his proper peer's title as Lord Kimbolton and also by his higher courtesy-title of Viscount Mandeville, son and heir-apparent of the Earl of Manchester. His first wife, who was a relative of the Duke of Buckingham, having died without issue, he had married, for his second, the Lady Anne Rich, daughter of the Earl of Warwick; and to this connection Clarendon ascribes, in great measure, his detachment from the Court-party, and his identification of himself with the Puritans. Certain it is that, through what is called the *Reign of Thorough*, the fact that Lord Kimbolton, the son of one of Charles's chief ministers, had abandoned his Court prospects and joined the ranks of the then suppressed Puritans, was much commented on, and that, in 1640, when the Scottish troubles compelled Charles again to summon an English Parliament, and the hopes of the Puritan party were thus revived, Kimbolton stepped forth as one of their chiefs. His activity and importance on the popular side in the first year of the struggle between the Long Parliament and the King were signally attested in January 1641-2, when he alone of the peers was conjoined by Charles, as Mr. Bruce mentions, with the five leading Commoners whose arrest Charles attempted in his famous and fatal *coup d'état*. Seven months afterwards, when the actual Civil War began (August 1642), it was natural that a nobleman already so distinguished should be one of the small body of about thirty peers who stood by Parliament at all risks, while the rest of their order, to the number of about one hundred, went with the King. He was then still only Lord Kimbolton or Viscount Mandeville; and he did not become Earl of Manchester till his father's death, November 7, 1642.—D.M.]

When King and Parliament adjourned the decision of the war of addresses and messages from Westminster to the tented field, Lord Manchester [still only Lord Kimbolton] took the command of a regiment of foot in the army of the Earl of Essex, and was present at the Battle of Edgehill.[a] He had not had any previous military experience; but, like other noblemen on both sides, he came forward at the commencement of the war as a leader in the field of the party which he espoused. [In a pamphlet, dated September 14, 1642, and entitled "*The List of the Army raised under the Command of his Excellency, Robert Earl of Essex,*" one of the twenty regiments of *Foot* of the Parliamentarian army at that date, each calculated at 1,200 men, is styled "Lord Mandeville's Regiment," Mandeville or Kimbolton himself taking rank as colonel of the regiment, with John Parkinson for his lieutenant-colonel, John Drake for his major, seven captains of companies under these, and Simeon Ashe as the regimental chaplain. Among the other colonels of Essex's foot regiments, each with his subordinate lieutenant-colonel, major, and captains, were the Earl of Stamford, Viscount Saye and Sele, Lord Wharton, Lord Brooke, and Lord Roberts, from the House of Lords, and Hampden and Denzil Holles from the House of Commons. The same list gives the *Horse* of Essex's army as divided into seventy-

---

[a] Fought on Sunday, October 23, 1642, near Keinton in South Warwickshire, the first important battle of the Civil War. The Parliament had, on the whole, the victory, though not a very decided one. Among the slain was Robert Bertie, Earl of Lindsey, commander-in-chief of the King's army.—D.M.

five troops of sixty men each. Of one of these troops, numbered the 67th, Oliver Cromwell, M.P. for Cambridge, was captain; and among the captains of other troops were several of the Parliamentarian peers and several of Cromwell's colleagues of the Lower House. But, superior to the mere captains of individual horse-troops, were six of their number, taking rank as colonels of horse: viz., the Earl of Bedford, Sir William Balfour, Lord Fielding, Lord Willoughby of Parham, Sir William Waller, and Edwin Sandys; besides whom there was a colonel of *Dragoons* in the person of John Browne, M.P. for Dorsetshire, commanding five troops of dragoons, each of 100 men, and each with its separate captain.—The relative military positions of the peer Lord Kimbolton and the commoner Oliver Cromwell in Essex's main Parliamentary army at the beginning of the Civil War may thus be easily conceived. Under Essex himself, as commander-in-chief, there were five chief officers ranking as *generals* (the Earl of Bedford and Sir William Balfour two of them); under these were 27 *colonels*, with about as many *lieutenant-colonels* and *majors;* and under these again were about 210 *captains* of foot, horse, and dragoons. Lord Kimbolton was one of the 27 colonels, commanding a foot regiment of 1200 men; Cromwell was one of the 210 captains, commanding a horse troop of 60 men. The captaincy of a troop of horse, however, was a somewhat higher thing in reputation than the captaincy of a company of foot.—Farther, it has to be noted that the above state of the army was little more than its state on paper at the outset, and that the first shocks and exigencies of the war greatly deranged the paper scheme. Officers that figure on the first paper list disappear, or even desert; others flash into note at once, and are promoted rapidly. It was not Essex alone that regulated the promotions; the Parliament was watching, and selected those that seemed fittest. Indeed, very soon there were other masses in the field in various parts of England, with the style of armies for the Parliament, besides Essex's main or original army, although Essex continued nominally the commander-in-chief.—D.M.]

When subsequently, in the year 1643, County Associations were formed, primarily for local defence, the Earl was put at the head of that one which comprised the Eastern Counties. In that capacity he came into direct military communication with Oliver Cromwell, whose regiment of Ironsides was principally raised and recruited in the county of Huntingdon, in which the Earl had great property and influence, and where he must have known Oliver Cromwell for many years.

[Mr. Bruce has here rapidly skipped the period of about fifteen months intervening between the Battle of Edgehill and the opening of the year 1644; but it seems necessary, for the understanding of what follows, that the reader should have some notice of the course of events during that interval, and especially of the steps by which Colonel Lord Kimbolton and Captain Oliver Cromwell had risen above their first ranks in the Parliamentary service.

After the Battle of Edgehill, the King, foiled in an attempted march upon London, had retired to Oxford, which became thenceforward his head-quarters; and through the winter of 1642-3, and the early summer of 1643, the war resolved itself into what may be called district-struggles, in which the Royalists and the Parliamentarians ascertained each other's strength by fights and sieges in the various parts of England, and, when any district had manifestly declared for the one side or the other, tried to keep it fast to that side by suppressing hostile risings within it, or repelling inroads from other districts. Rupert in the Midlands, Lord Herbert on the South-Welsh border, the Marquis of Hertford and Sir Ralph Hopton in the South-Western counties, and the Marquis of Newcastle in the North, were the Royalist chiefs most heard of; on the side of Parliament, Essex was still generalissimo, but with Sir William Waller as his most active lieutenant in the South, Earl Stamford and others in command in the South-West, and Lord Ferdinando Fairfax and his son Sir Thomas Fairfax doing their best in the North. On the whole, the military hero of the Parliament through those first few months of the war was Sir William Waller. His brilliant successes,

xii   HISTORICAL PREFACE.

first in the South-East and then in the West, contrasted favourably with Essex's heavy strategy, and suggested to some the idea that *he* might be the better commander-in-chief. For the rest all was dubious; nay, surveying the map of England, and observing that the King had a strong hold of the Midlands, with Wales behind him as one unbroken magazine of Royalism, the South-West counties as far as Cornwall almost wholly his, and the North tending to be his, one might have pronounced the chances to be greatly in his favour.

The strength of Parliament was mainly in the Eastern and South-Eastern counties, nearest London; and within that region the six eastern counties of Norfolk, Suffolk, Essex, Cambridge, Herts, and Hunts, had acquired especial distinction. Although, as Mr. Bruce mentions, the association of neighbouring counties into groups all over the map was part of the policy of the Parliament, and five or six such associations had sprung up in the winter of 1642-3 or early in 1643, the six counties named (five only at first, but Hunts was added) had come to be known as "The Associated Counties" *par excellence*. This was owing in a great measure to the energy and activity of Cromwell. As a native of the district, and as representative in Parliament of one of its chief towns, he had naturally begun his soldiering there, and proved there first, at the age of forty-three, his inborn military genius. From the very first, in raising the single Cambridgeshire horse-troop of which he was captain, he had proceeded instinctively on his famous principle of selecting "men with a spirit for the business," men like-minded religiously with himself; and gradually, after having himself learnt his drill, and drilled his first troop, he had applied the same principle with greater and greater confidence in recruiting that troop, and in raising others. Accordingly, in March, 1643, he was no longer "Captain Cromwell," but "Colonel Cromwell," at the head of a whole regiment of the sort of men that were afterwards known as Cromwell's Ironsides. The nominal head of the Eastern Counties Association was then Lord Grey of Wark; but the soul of the Association was Colonel

Cromwell. The particulars of his soldiering and miscellaneous activity from March to August, 1643—mostly at Cambridge or elsewhere within the Association, but with some important excursions beyond it, and especially one into Lincolnshire for the rescue of that county from risings of its native Royalist elements, aided by "infalls" of Royalists from the north—will be gathered best from Mr. Carlyle's narrative (*Letters and Speeches of Cromwell*, i. 103–132, ed. 1857).

Meanwhile in other parts of England the cause of Parliament had met with alarming disasters. The Fairfaxes had lost an important battle in the north; Sir William Waller, despatched into the south-western counties as the likeliest man to retrieve former failures there, had been twice beaten; the city of Bristol, insufficiently defended, had surrendered to Rupert. Under the pressure of these misfortunes the Parliament had resolved on what they had for some time contemplated, and had sent envoys to Edinburgh to solicit the armed aid of the Scots. Various changes of command were at the same time made within England itself, and among them one affecting the Eastern Counties. Lord Kimbolton, Earl of Manchester since November, 1642, had not ceased to be a star of the first magnitude among the few Parliamentarian peers; and he had been honoured as such in various ways, *e.g.*, in being nominated as one of the ten peers who were to sit as lay-members in the famous Assembly of Divines, convened at Westminster, July 1st, 1643, to advise the Parliament in ecclesiastical matters. His first great military command, however, dates from August, 1643. Lord Grey of Wark having, it appears, hardly satisfied either Cromwell or the Parliament in the discharge of his duty as head of the Associated Eastern Counties, the Earl of Manchester, whose connections with that district were in any case numerous and close, had been pitched upon as his successor in the post. "*Ordered*, that my Lord General (Essex) be desired to grant a commission to the Earl of Manchester to be Serjeant Major General of all the Forces of the Six Associated Counties," is the entry in the Commons Journals, under date

August 9, 1643; followed by this entry on the same day, "*Resolved*, that the Six Associated Counties shall raise 10,000 foot and dragoons to withstand the enemy."[a]

Cromwell and the Earl of Manchester had, of course, known each other well before this time; but their co-operation in the military service of the Parliament now first properly began.[b] The Earl was the commander-in-chief of the Associated Counties; Cromwell was one of four colonels under the Earl, with the governorship of the city of Ely just added to his colonelcy. But, whoever were the other three colonels, the foremost in council and in action was always Cromwell. This appears amply in the records that remain of the transactions from August, 1643, to January, 1643-4, in that section of the Civil War which included the Associated Counties

---

[a] The two extracts from the Commons Journals are not directly on my part from the Journals themselves, but from those sheets of miscellaneous MS. jottings, left by Mr. Bruce in connection with his unfinished Preface, which seem to me to prove that he meant, in completing his Preface, to make some such insertions and additions as have now to be made for him.—D.M.

[b] A story told by Clarendon in his *Life* (p. 936, ed. 1843) is worth noting here. Shortly after the meeting of the Long Parliament, and when Cromwell was a comparatively unknown man in it, a question of private grievance came before the House of Commons, relating to an inclosure of waste lands in the Eastern Counties. As the lands had been acquired by the old Earl of Manchester, Lord Privy Seal, it was his interest and that of his son, then Viscount Mandeville or Lord Kimbolton, to maintain the inclosure: the complainants, on the other hand, were tenant farmers in the district. Some of them had come up to town as witnesses; and in a private committee of the House on the subject Cromwell distinguished himself by marshalling the witnesses, seconding their statements, and seeing them get fair play. He was so "tempestuous" in his behaviour on the occasion that Mr. Hyde, who was chairman (*i.e.* Clarendon himself), had to call him to order and threaten to report him to the House. In especial he was "rude" to Lord Mandeville. "When, upon any matter of fact or the proceeding before and at the inclosure, the Lord Mandeville desired to be heard, and with great modesty related what had been done or explained what had been said, Mr. Cromwell did answer and reply upon him with so much indecency and rudeness, and in language so contrary and offensive, that every man would have thought that, as their natures and their manners were as opposite as it is possible, so their interest could never have been the same." Mandeville himself, now Earl of Manchester, does not seem to have remembered this encounter with Mr. Cromwell half so bitterly as Mr. Hyde did for him.—D.M.

(see Carlyle's *Cromwell*, i. 132-146, ed. 1857). Much of the work consisted in urging on the levies of the new forces that had been ordered; but the feat of greatest mark was the complete recovery of Lincolnshire. That county had continued to be the debateable land between the Parliamentarians of the Eastern Counties and the Royalists of the North under the Marquis of Newcastle; and the question was whether Newcastle, who had driven the Fairfaxes into the very south of Yorkshire and was besieging Lord Fairfax in Hull, should be able to cross the Humber, annex all Lincolnshire to the Royalist area, and so break in upon the Eastern Counties, or whether Manchester, with Cromwell under him, and with the aid of Sir Thomas Fairfax, who had brought his horse across the Humber for the purpose, should be able to make Lincolnshire good and so repel the invasion. It was virtually decided by the Fight of Winceby, October 11, 1643, in which, mainly by Cromwell's exertions, the Lincolnshire Royalists, and the Northern Royalists who had broken in to assist them, were utterly beaten. The county was then cleared of the intruders; and, the Marquis of Newcastle having raised the siege of Hull and withdrawn farther back into Yorkshire, it was plain that he had been foiled in his hope of carrying the stress of the war into the Eastern Counties and would have to abide it in his own North.

Of what importance this result appeared to the Parliament may be inferred from this entry in the Commons Journals, Nov. 6, 1643: "*Ordered*, that Sir Peter Wentworth and Sir Anthony Irby do present unto the Earl of Manchester the thanks of this House in acknowledgement of the great services done by him to the Commonwealth."[a] Thenceforward, in fact, Manchester, though still in terms of his commission only serjeant-major-general for the Associated Counties by deputation from Essex, was regarded as an independent general-in-chief at the head of one of the sectional armies of the Parliament, while for Cromwell the consequence was that he

---

[a] I find this extract from the Commons Journals in Mr. Bruce's miscellaneous jottings, and I copy it from them.—D.M.

ceased to be merely Colonel Cromwell (though that name is found occasionally attached to him for some time longer in contemporary documents) and became Manchester's second, or lieutenant-general, in the same sectional army.— D.M.]

In January 1643-4 Oliver Cromwell gave clear evidence that up to that time he had acted in harmony with Lord Manchester. Himself ever active and fearless in the public service, he was the plain-spoken exposer of the incompetency of others. Lord Willoughby [of Parham] was the commander (serjeant-major-general was the official title) of the troops raised by the county of Lincoln for the Association of the Eastern Counties. He * * * *

[There is a gap here in Mr. Bruce's manuscript; but it is not difficult to judge how he would have filled it up.

The Parliamentarian Lord-Lieutenant for the county of Lincoln since the beginning of the war had been Francis, Lord Willoughby of Parham, already mentioned as one of the six colonels of horse in Essex's original army.[a] To strengthen his hands, he had, as Mr. Bruce has just said, been also commissioned by Essex as General of the Lincolnshire forces. Hence in the struggle, just described, between the Northern Royalists and the Parliamentarians of the Eastern Counties for the possession of Lincolnshire, Lord Willoughby had been a man of some significance, and Manchester, Cromwell, and Sir Thomas Fairfax had been brought into relations with him.[b] Cromwell, in particular, had found reason for thinking him a very incompetent person for his post; and, accordingly, when the immediate business was over, and Cromwell had leisure to run up to London and appear transiently in his place in Parliament, he is found "complaining much of my Lord Willoughby, as of a backward general, with strangely dissolute people about him, a great sorrow to Lincolnshire, and craving that my Lord Manchester might be appointed there instead."[c] This was on the 22nd of

---

[a] See Rushworth, v. 108-109, and p. x. *ante.*—D.M.
[b] Rushworth, v. 280.—D.M.
[c] Carlyle's *Cromwell*, i. 146, ed. 1857.—D.M.

January, 1643-4 ; and on that very day, it appears from the Commons Journals, it was ordered by the Commons "that the Lord General (Essex) be desired to grant the Earl of Manchester a commission to be Major-General of co. Lincoln."[a] In other words, Lord Willoughby was deprived of the military command of Lincolnshire, and, by the addition of that county to the six Associated Eastern Counties, the Association over which Manchester presided, and in which Cromwell was his Lieutenant-General, was extended over seven counties. Willoughby fiercely resented his disgrace, and even sent a challenge to Manchester. Various entries in the Lords and Commons Journals, in February 1643-4, show that the two Houses interfered to compose matters, and that Cromwell was regarded as the mainspring of the affair.[b] Altogether, Mr. Bruce is quite justified in citing the affair as a distinct proof that in January, 1643-4, there was a thoroughly cordial understanding between Manchester and Cromwell. There are other proofs to the same effect. In fact, Cromwell had hitherto found Manchester a chief with whom he could *get on*, because, in all essentials, he could *manage* him.

Farther to supply the missing links at this point of Mr. Bruce's narrative, we must extend the view a little:—Essex, as generalissimo for Parliament, had remained characteristically sluggish throughout the year 1643. The siege and capture of Reading in April, and a successful march westwards in August and September for the relief of Gloucester, followed by something like a victory over the King's main army in the first Battle of Newbury (Sept. 20), had been the sum of his exploits in that year. Discontented with such barren strategy, though full of respect for Essex,

---

[a] This quotation from the Commons Journals is from Mr. Bruce's own jottings.—D.M.

[b] In Mr. Bruce's miscellaneous jottings I find several extracts from the Lords Journals relating to Willoughby's dispute with Manchester. They need not be reproduced here ; but they show Mr. Bruce's care in collecting materials for the perfection of his Preface.—D.M.

it had become the policy of Parliament more and more to distribute the responsibility among the leaders of sectional armies, nominally deriving their commissions from Essex, but really with independent powers and chances. About the time when the Earl of Manchester had been set up in his serjeant-major-generalship or command-in-chief in the Eastern Counties (Aug. 1643), Essex had been persuaded, though not without some difficulty and show of offended dignity, to grant a similar major-generalship, in the form of the command-in-chief of a new army to be raised by the Londoners, to his rival Sir William Waller.[a] Thus at the close of 1643 and beginning of 1644 one may say that there were four Parliamentary armies in England, besides garrisons and local forces —Essex's own main army ; Waller's, raised or to be raised, also for action chiefly in the south and west ; Manchester's, of the seven Associated Eastern Counties; and the army of the Fairfaxes in the north. But by the end of January 1643-4, lo! a *fifth* army available. It was no other than that auxiliary army of Scots which had been applied for in the preceding August. All arrangements having been made with the Scottish Government, and the two nations having sworn a strict alliance on the basis of the *Solemn League and Covenant*, binding them to mutual defence and the endeavour after a uniformity of religion and Church government, this army had at last entered England, wading through the snow, 21,000 strong, with the Earl of Leven for its chief, and Lieutenant-General William Baillie and Major-General David Leslie next in command.

With the advent of the Scottish army came, almost necessarily,

[a] This incident also had been noted by Mr. Bruce, probably for use in his Preface had he perfected it. I find among his jottings several extracts from the Commons Journals, from July to Sept. 1643 inclusively, relating to the proposition of a separate command for Sir William Waller and to Essex's reluctance in the matter from personal pride or from jealousy of Waller. At length, it is reported (Sept. 28), Essex is pacified, and handsomely assures the House that he " will begin upon a new score, and give Waller the best encouragement he can."—D.M.

a new modification of the system of the war, trenching farther on the powers of Essex. Two independent nations being now conjoined in a common enterprise, it was thought fitting that there should be a central body consisting of representatives of both, to direct the generals and correspond with them; and this was provided by the institution (Feb. 16, 1643-4) of what was called THE COMMITTEE OF BOTH KINGDOMS. It consisted, for the English Parliament, of seven selected Peers and fourteen selected Commoners, and, for the Scottish Government, of four Commissioners that had accompanied the Scottish army. Essex, Manchester, Sir William Waller, and Cromwell were of the English part of this Committee, and the same compliment was paid to others in military posts; but, as effectively the Committee was to have its *habitat* in London and to issue its directions thence, the working core of it was to be a small quorum, chiefly of civilians (six from the two English Houses, but always with two Scots present), who could be resident in London and in daily communication with Parliament. As Derby House, in Cannon Row, Westminster, became the meeting-place of this Committee, it received the name of the COMMITTEE AT DERBY HOUSE; and under this name, as well as under the other, it was, with renewals and modifications from time to time, to be a very important executive body in England, in the guise of a war-office, for several years to come. Essex by no means liked the new institution, but he had to acquiesce.

The particular army with which we have meanwhile to do is Manchester's army of the Seven Associated Eastern Counties. It consisted of about 14,000 foot, horse, and dragoons;[a] it had already acquired great reputation; and much was expected from it. At its head was the Earl of Manchester, a popular Puritan nobleman, forty-one years of age at the opening of 1644; his lieutenant-general was Oliver Cromwell, three years older.—D.M.]

Such were the persons with whom we have to deal, and such their relative positions. Manchester was the commander-in-chief,

[a] Rushworth, v. 621.—D.M.

Cromwell the second in command: Manchester, described by Bishop Burnet, in words which singularly confirm and illustrate those of Clarendon, as " of a soft and obliging temper, of no great depth, but universally beloved, being both a virtuous and a generous man;"[a] Cromwell, a soldier such as the world was then beginning to know him, all fire and intensity; never allowing an enemy near him to be at rest, and carrying on his troops from success to success until they partook of his own enthusiasm; believing himself to be fighting the Lord's battles, and doing so at the head of men who held the same faith and felt the same scorn of danger as himself—

> All that the contest calls for,—spirit, strength,
> The scorn of danger, and united hearts,—
> The surest presage of the good they seek.
> COWPER. Task, v. 366-68.

In the affairs of this world it has not yet become possible for the lion and the lamb to lie down together. It is even less wonderful that the combination was out of the question in the case of Cromwell and the Earl of Manchester, inasmuch as the Earl's major-general, the next officer to Cromwell in command, " helped " his two superiors, in the language of Mr. Carlyle, " to quarrel." Crawford, the major-general, was a Scotchman of good descent, and was full of his country's warm attachment to Presbyterianism and the Covenant. Cromwell had little affection either for Scotland or its institutions.

[Some additional information seems here desirable, and would probably have been given by Mr. Bruce.

Notwithstanding the great accession of strength which the Parliament had received by the coming in of Leven's auxiliary army of Scots, there was a decided lull of military activity in the early months of 1644. That army had duly quartered itself in the north in aid of that of the Fairfaxes; and there were minor move-

---

[a] *Hist. of Own Time*, i. 167, ed. 1823. Baillie terms the Earl " a sweet, meek man."—*Letters*, ii. 229.

ments and detached pieces of service of the other armies, including an expedition of Cromwell westward as far as Gloucester; but there were no great operations. The cause may have been that the King, whom the advent of the Scots had alarmed, was then holding an Anti-Parliament or Royalist Parliament in Oxford (January 22, 1643-4—April 16, 1644), and there was talk of a possible peace. At all events, Manchester had leisure for a while for other duties than those of his generalship: *e.g.*, for some actual attendances in his place in the Westminster Assembly, and then for that great business of the visitation and reformation of the University of Cambridge which Parliament had assigned to him by special ordinance as a work of supreme importance within the territories he administered. From February, through March and April, 1644, he and his chaplains, Messrs. Ashe and Goode, were at Cambridge, busy in this work, *i.e.*, summoning heads and fellows of colleges before them, examining the states of the colleges, ejecting men of the wrong sort from their masterships or fellowships, and putting into their places Puritan ministers and scholars recommended by the Westminster Assembly. As Cromwell for part of this time was also at Cambridge, he and Manchester must have been often together, Cromwell looking sympathetically upon Manchester's doings in the University, but in the main occupying himself with the duties of his lieutenant-generalship, and getting the army of the Associated Counties ready for further service in the war when Manchester should resume command.

By this time, however, there was a third person of influence in that army, somewhat disturbing the relations that had hitherto subsisted between Manchester and Cromwell. Since the coming-in of the Scottish auxiliary army, stray Scots, willing to be employed in one or other of the English armies proper, had been even more plentiful than before; and one of these Scots had been picked up by Manchester, or had been recommended to him, as a fit man to be his major-general. He was the "Crawford" of whom Mr. Bruce speaks: Laurence Crawford, of the family of the Crawfords of Jordan Hill, Renfrewshire.[a] He had seen service both abroad and in Scotland, and it may have been thought that his trained professional ability would be a useful importation into Manchester's army, led otherwise only by an English nobleman and an English gentleman-farmer who had turned soldiers for the nonce. But from the moment of this importation peace was gone, and the management of Manchester's army became a very difficult case of the problem of three bodies. This was largely owing to the peculiar temperament of Crawford, who "paints himself to us," says Mr. Carlyle, " as a headlong audacious fighter, of loose loud tongue, much of a pedant and braggart, somewhat given to sycophancy too;"[b] but, as Mr. Bruce has hinted, and as Mr. Carlyle also has occasion to show, the difference between Crawford and Cromwell involved questions of theology and ecclesiastical polity then much agitating the mind of England. Cromwell was a fervid English Puritan of the largest-hearted type, whose very principle in selecting his Ironsides was that they should be religious men, having what he thought "the root of the matter in them," but who, when he was sure of that, cared little for formal differences, and even valued liberty of difference. Crawford was a man of the most narrow and pragmatic type of the Scottish Puritanism of that day, a rigid believer in strict Scottish Presbytery as the one and only true religious discipline in the world: by no means a stalwart Dalgetty, placidly adjusting himself to any medium, but an irascible martinet for orthodoxy.

Care must be taken, however, not to misapprehend, in connection with this contrast, Mr. Bruce's phrases "Presbyterianism and the Covenant," and "Scotland or its institutions." Scotland had then

---

[a] Douglas's *Baronage of Scotland*, i. 430. From Crawford himself we learn that he joined Manchester's army in February 1643-4: see his narrative among the documents in this volume, p. 59. Care must be taken not to confound this "Major-General Laurence Crawford" with another Scottish "Crawford," who will appear in the course of the story.—D.M.

[b] Carlyle's *Cromwell*, i. 150, ed. 1857.—D.M.

two Covenants, distinct in their aims and in their wording—the *National Scottish Covenant* of 1638, under the banner of which she had fought her own quarrel with Charles I., and succeeded in re-Presbyterianizing herself; and the *Solemn League and Covenant* of 1643, which, though it was of Scottish origin, was not a peculiarly Scottish institution, inasmuch as it had been adopted enthusiastically by the English Parliament as the fittest bond of union between the two nations, and signed universally by the English Parliamentarians on the one hand as well as by the Scots on the other. In respect of the latter, Cromwell, as one of the myriads of Englishmen who had signed that covenant, was no less a " Covenanter " than Crawford was; nor had any sign appeared yet on Cromwell's part, or among those he represented, of a desire to disown or repudiate that covenant. Very distinctly, however, had signs by this time appeared of a difference in the interpretation of the document. The Scots viewed it as implying that strict Presbytery, with no toleration of anything else, was to be set up in England; they had sent their auxiliary army into England as an agency to that end; and, as the Londoners and the majority of the English Parliamentarians everywhere had caught the passion for Presbyterianism, they were in prospect of success. An unascertained minority of the Parliamentarians, however, had by no means made up their minds that Scottish Presbytery would be the best form of established Church government for England, and had very decidedly made up their minds that, if such an establishment should be set up, there should be at least a toleration of dissent and liberty for varieties of worship under it. True, there were phrases in the *Solemn League and Covenant* pledging its subscribers to " endeavour to bring the Churches of God in the three kingdoms to the nearest conjunction and uniformity in religion," and also to " endeavour the extirpation of popery, prelacy, superstition, heresy, schism, and profaneness;" but were Englishmen to be tied down already to that Scottish interpretation of these phrases which would dictate the acceptance of Scottish Presbytery in all its details as the only " conjunction and uniformity" possible, and would propose civil pains and penalties on all that the Scots called " heretics " or " schismatics " as the only way of extirpating real " heresy " and real " schism"? Already, in the beginning of 1644, this difference as to the interpretation of the Covenant was a growing one; and, when Crawford entered Manchester's army, he imported into it not only his own peevish temper but also the Scottish construction of the obligations of the Covenant. By that construction it was the duty of all in high command in any of the Parliamentary armies to see that heresy did not break out in the ranks, and especially that the officers were orthodox. Hardly, in fact, had Crawford become major-general in the army of the Eastern Counties, when, as Mr. Bruce goes on to relate, an instance in point occurred.—D.M.]

The lieutenant-colonel of Crawford's regiment [a Lieutenant-Colonel Packer.—D.M.] having given him offence [near Bedford, Manchester and Cromwell being then both at Cambridge.—D. M.] was placed by him under arrest [and then sent back to Cambridge, as a suspended officer, until Manchester should be at leisure to investigate the case.—D.M.] The culprit, whose general character was good, appealed to Cromwell, who interceded by letter to Crawford on his behalf. [The letter, written at Cambridge and dated 10th March 1643-4, was carried by Packer himself to Crawford, then in Buckinghamshire.—D.M.] To his special offence the lieutenant-colonel added that of being an Anabaptist. " Admit he be," remarked Cromwell, " shall that render him incapable to serve the public ? . . . . Sir, the State, in choosing men to serve it, takes no notice of their opinions: if they be willing faithfully to serve it, that satisfies. I advised you formerly to bear with men of different minds from yourself. . . . Take heed of being sharp, or too easily sharpened by others, against those to whom you can object little but that they square not with you in every opinion concerning matters of religion."[a]

[a] Carlyle's *Cromwell*, i. 201, ed. 1846 [i. 147-148, ed. 1857.]

It took nearly two centuries to make such opinions as these of Cromwell to be generally admitted. In his time politicians denounced them as highly dangerous, and divines as peculiarly wicked.[a] Manchester, stirred up by Crawford, who had "a great hand with him,"[b] was strong against them; and hence a source of strife between Cromwell and his commander-in-chief.[c]

Nor was the strife upon this subject simply theoretical, or one which in practice affected only a particular person, like this Lieutenant-Colonel, here and there. At that time the question of the rights of sectaries was really vital. It determined the whole course of public policy.

At the commencement of the war between King and Parliament, the people prepared for it as for a mere demonstration of strength,

[a] Somewhat too strongly stated. There was a considerable number of persons in England in 1644, including some politicians and some divines, who had conceived as wide and just ideas of toleration as any that have been generally admitted since ; and Cromwell was but the most conspicuous public head of these, and their most emphatic spokesman.—D.M.

[b] Baillie's Letters, ii. 229.

[c] Mr. Bruce seems here to anticipate a little. At the date at which we now are (March 1644), it cannot be said that the strife between Cromwell and Manchester had begun, but only that an influence leading to strife had been introduced between them in the person of Crawford. In that letter of Cromwell's from which Bruce has quoted (see the whole of it in Carlyle's *Cromwell*, i. 147-8, ed. 1857) there is no sign of any idea on the part of Cromwell that Manchester would have differed from him, or sided with Crawford, in the case of Packer. Manchester was then too busy, he says, with the University Visitation to hear what Packer had to say in self-defence ; but it seems to be implied that Cromwell, in writing the letter, could assume that he and Manchester would be of one mind on the "Anabaptist" objection. Not till afterwards, when gradually Crawford had acquired his "great hand" with Manchester, is there any reason for characterising Manchester as "strong against" those Toleration opinions of Cromwell which, till Crawford's advent, he seems to have abetted, or at least allowed to Cromwell in the recruiting and officering of the Ironsides. Possibly, however, his recent sittings in the Westminster Assembly, and his communications with that body in the business of new appointments in the University, may have given him a turn already towards Presbyterian strictness, and so prepared the way for Crawford's insinuations against Cromwell.—D.M.

or at most as for a contest in the arena. So badly had the King's friends managed their cause, so little show had they made of their real strength, that it was a common opinion that one battle would end the struggle, that a victory clearly pronounced on either side would bring the long-continued strife of words to an end. This opinion was soon shown to be fallacious. The new course entered upon when the King raised his standard [Aug. 1642] turned out to be, not a battle, but a war. Still there were many persons on the side of the Parliament, including the anti-royal leaders of the highest social position, who went on dreaming that all that was needed was a war of resistance. If they could but make such a stand against the King as would convince him that he could no more overpower them by arms than by the measures to which he had previously had recourse, they imagined that he would submit to the curtailments of his prerogative and the other alterations in Church and State which they had determined to effect.

Such persons neither understood the character of the King nor the necessary course of such a war. Party bitterness grew with what it fed upon. It was strengthened by every victory and every defeat, by every loss and every sacrifice. The relative positions of the parties also gradually changed. The Parliament, with a view to the maintenance of their own position, was compelled to assume, within the portion of the kingdom which was under its control, first one and then another of the functions of the executive. At the end of two years (which is the period with which we are now dealing) they had appointed lord-lieutenants and sheriffs, they had made arrangements for the administration of justice, they had impressed soldiers, had levied taxes, had held direct communications with foreign governments, had made a separate treaty with the Scots, and had called them into England to their military assistance. The contest was no longer between two co-ordinate powers in one system of government; it had become a war between two bodies each of whom exercised an independent and sovereign jurisdiction, a war which could only be what the King had all along designed it to be, not merely one of defence, nor of resistance, but simply and absolutely a war of conquest.

This was a lesson which the original Parliamentary leaders were slow to learn. From the meeting of the Long Parliament they had consistently pursued certain definite aims, settled probably, in general terms, among themselves before the Parliament assembled. They had determined I. To punish the evil counsellors who had advised and assisted the King in his course of arbitrary government; II. To secure frequent meetings of Parliament; III. To reform the Courts of Law, which had been perverted to purposes of oppression; IV. To effect such a reform in the Church as should prevent a fresh intrusion of Laudism. Whilst they were pursuing these objects in a parliamentary way, the conduct of the King compelled them for their own safety sake to add a Vth object to their programme, namely, To secure a temporary parliamentary control over the militia; and the war added a VIth, To exclude from future power and influence those who had been the King's principal military supporters.

The first three of these objects were accomplished and the fourth and fifth were under discussion when the standard was raised. The sixth could only receive its determination at the close of the war. The fourth touched the conscience of the King, and the fifth his pride. But he had yielded to the Scots [in their struggle with him for the re-establishment of Presbytery in Scotland, 1638–1640.—D.M.]; he had yielded [in England] in the case of triennial parliaments, and in that of Strafford [1641]; and there was ground for hope that he might be induced to do so in other things. The case of the Militia seemed peculiarly susceptible of diplomatic arrangement. Combination of authority and limitation of time were bases upon which arbitrators might work. Even the Church question did not seem entirely insoluble. The consent of the King to the removal of the Bishops from the House of Lords [Feb. 1641-2] was a great concession to popular opinion, but it was made too late. In the first instance that and some other modifications of the hierarchical government would have sufficed. Even to a late period, if the King had stood his ground, and the powerful friends of Episcopacy had honestly contested the matter in parliament, a peaceful settlement might have been come to. The war put an end to the possibility of arrangement. Thenceforward the changes effected by Parliament were in most instances the results of the necessities of their political position. Presbyterianism was substituted in the place of Episcopacy as a sacrifice to the league with Scotland. There was indeed a large and influential party in England that desired Presbyterianism in lieu of Episcopacy. The existence of such a party is a necessary reaction against Laudism; but that party would have consented to a modified Episcopacy, and it was simply the general anxiety to secure the military assistance of the Scots which drove the Parliament into the adoption of this great organic change.

[Some correction of Mr. Bruce's language is here necessary:— The " great organic change " of which he speaks, viz., the substitution of Presbyterianism for Episcopacy in the National Church of England, had *not* been accomplished at the date he has reached in his narrative. The exclusion of bishops from the House of Lords and from other places of secular authority and jurisdiction had been carried, and assented to by the King, in Feb. 1641-2, six months before the beginning of the Civil War; various other acts and resolutions relating to the Church had since then been passed by the two Houses, amounting in the gross to an utter abolition of the Episcopal form of Church government, root and branch; and this fact had been put on record in the ordinance of the two Houses, June 12, 1643, convoking the Westminster Assembly of Divines.

Whereas it has been declared and resolved by the Lords and Commons assembled in Parliament that the present Church government by Archbishops, Bishops, their Chancellors, Commissaries, Deans, Deans and Chapters, Archdeacons, and other ecclesiastical officers depending on the hierarchy, is evil, and greatly offensive and burdensome to the kingdom, and a great impediment to reformation and growth of religion, and very prejudicial to the State and Government of this kingdom, and that therefore they are resolved that the same shall be taken away, and that such a government shall be settled in the Church as may be agreeable to God's Holy Word, and most apt to procure and preserve the peace of the Church at home, and nearer agreement with the Church of Scotland, and other Reformed Churches abroad :—

Such is part of the preamble of this ordinance, and the ordinance itself goes on to entrust to about 150 persons named, divines and others, the business of deliberating such questions as to the future constitution and standards of the Church as may be expressly referred to them by Parliament, and of advising Parliament in the same. When the Westminster Assembly did meet (July 1, 1643) it was pretty clear that the drift of opinion among the active majority of the members was towards Presbyterianism, and indeed it was afterwards maintained that the members had been selected by the two Houses beforehand with a view to that result; but not till after the *Solemn League and Covenant* had been made with the Scots, and some Scottish divines and laymen had been added to the Assembly as assessors to the English members, was the Assembly empowered to begin the consideration of the form of Church government to be substituted for Episcopacy (Oct. 1643). Then, partly in consequence of the enthusiasm over the new compact with the Scots, and of the presence of Henderson and other Scottish divines in the Assembly, the preponderance of Presbyterian opinion in that body was overwhelming—only five English divines, called "the Dissenting Brethren," questioning the Presbyterian theory of a Church, and putting in arguments in favour of the rival theory known as Congregationalism or Independency. Always outvoted in the debates, these five Dissenters at length changed their tactics. Knowing Presbytery to be predetermined on in the Assembly, and that a decisive recommendation in favour of that form of Church government would go from the Assembly to Parliament, they started a side-question, and openly appealed on this question both to Parliament and to the general public (Jan. 1643-4). This was the question of Toleration.

If Presbytery were to be set up in England, as seemed now certain, was it to be an absolute Presbytery, compulsory on every man, woman, and child; or would some allowance be made for tender consciences that could not reconcile themselves to all the details of the Established Church, and would ministers like themselves be permitted to preach in a peaceful non-Presbyterian way to such congregations as might voluntarily gather round them? Such was still the state of the controversy at the point Mr. Bruce has reached in his narrative, viz., March or April 1644. The establishment of Presbytery had not yet been actually voted in England, nor did the formal votes to that effect pass Parliament till the following year; it was only *as good as voted*, or *certain to be voted*.

In view of this, however, there was an enormous agitation of the whole mind of the country. The very air was full of new questions and new phrases. Now first did most Englishmen hear of the dispute between PRESBYTERY and INDEPENDENCY, and learn what it was all about. Presbyterian divines, both English and Scottish, put forth pamphlets upon pamphlets, explaining the Presbyterian system, *i.e.*, that system in which, while each parish or congregation has its own Church Court, consisting of the minister and lay elders, yet, for the purposes of control and unity, there must be a regular gradation of superior judicatories, called the *Presbytery* or *Classis* (the District Court, supervising a group of congregations), the *Provincial Synod* (the periodical court of a whole shire or of several shires, supervising all the Presbyteries within its bounds), and the *General Assembly* (the annual or occasional meeting of representative ministers and lay elders for the whole nation). They demonstrated the divine origin of this system, and its adaptation to human society; and they pointed to Scotland as an example of its admirable working. The five Dissenting Brethren and their allies, on the other hand, put forth pamphlets maintaining the divine origin and the superior freedom of *Congregationalism*, the main principle of which is the " independency " of individual congregations, though it admits the utility of correspondence between different congregations and occasional meetings for consultation. With the main question as between the two systems, however, was blended that side question of Toleration which the Dissenting Brethren had started. Would the Presbyterians, while establishing their system, concede some amount of toleration under it? One cannot now perceive any necessary or logical reason, inherent in the nature of the Presbyterian system of Church government, why they should not have agreed to do so; and it might be a curious speculation what would have happened if they had so agreed. Had the English and Scottish Presbyterians in 1644 consented to set up Presbytery *with* a toleration, how the future course of English history might have been changed! In fact, they would hear of nothing of the kind. Absolute, universal, strict, compulsory Presbytery was their sole idea of Presbytery; toleration or liberty of conscience, name or thing, much or little, was their bugbear, their horror, the condensation in one phrase of all that was hideous, abominable, and to be resisted. In other words, anti-toleration was proclaimed as a necessary tenet of true Presbyterianism. All the more naturally the doctrine of liberty of conscience became precious to the small minority of English parliamentarian divines who had adopted the theory of Congregationalism or Independency, and to the scattered thousands of persons throughout England who, for the same or for other reasons, looked forward with dread to the substitution of absolute Presbytery for the Prelacy that had been abolished. Nay, the interpretation of the phrase " liberty of conscience " grew bolder and bolder.—D.M.]

When it [*i. e.* the virtual adoption of Presbytery in lieu of the abolished Episcopacy, though with the question of Toleration in reserve.—D.M.] was accomplished, the old leaders of the movement party had finished their contemplated work of rational reformation. They were not blind, we may feel well assured, to the inconveniences and irregularities attendant upon their hasty legislation. But, satisfied with what they esteemed to be their clear gain in having got rid of an intolerant hierarchy based upon Popish principles, fondly attached to Popish ceremonies, and animated by a Popish spirit, they trusted to time and to subsequent limitations and qualifications to accommodate the change to the customs and notions of the English people.

Such feelings brought them necessarily into strong harmony with the popular desire for peace. The miseries of the war which had desolated the country for a couple of years had excited in the minds of the timid and the restless an ardent longing for the close of the unnatural strife. These feelings were forced upon the attention of the Parliament by the representations of excited multitudes; and, although such men as Essex, Northumberland, and Manchester in the one house, and [Holles, Stapleton, and Whitlocke] in the other, neither partook in the despondency nor the mutability of the populace, they might well feel that, having revised all the great establishments of the kingdom and accomplished such legislative changes as indicated that England of the Future which they desired, and having secured such military assistance as gave them a clear superiority in the field, the time had come for an earnest and urgent endeavour to put an end to the pending anarchy by an arrangement with their unwilling sovereign. Nor was there absent from their minds another feeling which urged them still more strongly to desire a peace. What evils might result from such a decided superiority of either party as would enable it to dictate terms of submission to its conquered adversaries! Such an ascendancy, on whichever side it occurred, would be followed by forfeitures and proscription, and would probably alter all the institutions of the country. Considerations like these led them to favour a military policy of exhaustion rather than of conquest. Such a policy was exemplified in the heavy inactivity of Essex. It discouraged audacity and enterprise. It opposed the recklessness of Rupert by steadiness, fortitude, and discretion. By such a policy it was hoped that the resources of the King would be exhausted, and he would be compelled to yield to England that freedom in relation to ecclesiastical affairs which had already been extorted from him by the Scots.

In the meantime a party was growing up which took a totally
different view of the position of affairs, both political and religious.
When they found victory followed by sluggishness and consequently
yielding small or no results, when the destruction of one royalist
army was succeeded by a period of inactivity which enabled the
King to form another, these men began to exclaim, " Shall the
sword devour for ever?" They chimed in with those whose
anxiety was for peace, but they sought it, not by outcry, nor by
vainer endeavours to come to terms with an opponent who refused
to admit the constitutional *status* of those with whom he treated,
but by directing all the national energies to obtain a victorious
close of the war. They accepted the issue offered by the King and
threw upon him the responsibility of the result. As means to their
end they advocated discipline and intelligence among the troops,
unity in command, activity in operations, and improvement to the
very utmost of all opportunities. In these views they had many
supporters, but the leading advocates of these opinions were men
who went much farther. They had no desire that the King should
close with the terms that were now offered to him, which comprised
the substitution of Presbyterianism for Episcopacy. Both these
schemes of ecclesiastical government claimed a foundation *jure
divino*. This party denied the foundation, and found no shelter
against past grievances in the substitution of the one scheme for
the other. They aimed at procuring what was then termed freedom
of conscience, a modified toleration of sectaries within a certain pale—
the first ray of the fuller light that has since risen upon ourselves;[a]

---

[a] Mr. Bruce is not absolutely right in describing the doctrine of Toleration that
had appeared in English society in 1644 as merely "the first ray of the fuller light
that has since risen upon ourselves." There were very various grades of the
doctrine even then; and, though most of the respectable people who advocated
Toleration did only mean "a modified toleration of sectaries within a certain pale,"
there were some thinkers whose notions of Toleration were as wide and exceptionless
as any that have since been known. Indeed Voluntaryism in its utmost extreme, as
denying the right of the civil power to establish, endow, patronise, or in any way
favour any form of religious belief, or interfere with any mis-belief or no-belief, was
then a proclaimed speculation.—D.M.

and in that particular they were most unpopular. But the point in which the popular voice went with them helped them on in spite of its union with that which was disliked, and so it was that they made way, and were shielded from the obloquy which, had they stood only upon the latter point, might possibly have overwhelmed them. Among their leaders it is scarcely necessary to remark that Oliver Cromwell was pre-eminent.

They who would picture to themselves Oliver Cromwell, at the period in which we have here to deal with him, must regard him not merely as a man whose actions were controlled by a strong, determined will, nor merely as a soldier strict in discipline, distinguished at all times by steady energy, in decision prompt, in execution unwavering. All these unquestionably he was, and probably those who did not know him the most intimately described him over and above as cold, reserved, unfeeling; but these things would scarcely have constituted a difference between Cromwell and multitudes of other resolute and peremptory men. He was much more. In him there was not merely a pre-determined judgment upon the points in dispute, but one which he believed to be infallible, because communicated to his mind by the Spirit of God. Call it enthusiasm, cant, fanaticism, hypocrisy, or what you will. He saw God's Church defiled by hirelings. He witnessed how they strove to bring back within the sacred precincts the soul-destroying trumpery of rejected superstitions. They who profaned God's Church could not be otherwise than enemies of the Lord of Hosts. To oppose them was the cause of God. It was in this cause, uniting the hero with the prophet, that he drew his sword; and, whenever his efforts were triumphant, he devoutly believed the success to be a token of God's approval—the flashing of his sword to be the lightning of God's vengeance.

* * * * *

These were the principles which he inculcated upon his Ironsides, and they in their turn, as much by their good conduct as by their achievements, made disciples and proselytes wherever they went, and that in spite of the angry opposition of Scots, of Presbyterians, of all who desired a royal restoration upon any terms, and of those who were alarmed at the multitude of enthusiastic sectaries who sprang up upon the removal of the over-stringent restraints of the Established Church. The sudden withdrawal of a rigorous religious system is always followed by an outburst of irregular enthusiasm. So it was at the Reformation, so on the occasion with which we are now dealing, and so it always will be. In the present instance the effects must have been greatly heightened by the unwise conduct of the Parliament in abolishing the Episcopal Government without substituting anything in its place for a considerable time. The Cavaliers commented as if with satisfaction upon those wild explosions of religious passion. They had no cause to do so. Persons thus affected kept the Ironsides at their full complement, and wherever they were found were the deadliest enemies of the royal cause.

[He would be a rash person that should try to complete an unfinished character of Cromwell by any one else, whether for 1644 or for any other epoch of Cromwell's life; and so Mr. Bruce's remarks on Cromwell have been left with his asterisks after them to denote their incompleteness. There is evidence, however, in the peculiarly fragmentary state of the manuscript at this point, that Mr. Bruce proposed additions in the way of fact that should farther illustrate the division into two parties that had appeared among the Parliamentarians in 1644, and Cromwell's pre-eminence in one of the parties. What is deficient may perhaps be supplied as follows:—

As Mr. Bruce has pointed out, there had even from the first been virtually two parties among the Parliamentarians, a more moderate and a more thoroughgoing. Whether one belonged to the one or to the other was partly an affair of natural temperament, partly of social rank and circumstances, partly of the intensity of acquired conviction beforehand on the political and religious questions at issue in the war. Most of the stately Parliamentarian lords, many of the members of the House of Commons, and a large following of the people, wanted to beat the King sufficiently, but not to beat him too much; they wanted to make such terms with him as would permit English society to resume its course, with royalty under due Parliamentary check, and the Church reformed and popularized, but other institutions disturbed as little as possible. Some of the more energetic spirits of both Houses, however, such as Viscount Saye and Sele and Lord Brooke in the Lords, and Hampden, Cromwell, Haselrig, the younger Sir Henry Vane, and Henry Marten, in the Commons, had no faith in any method of bringing the King to terms short of his crushing defeat in the field, and did not shrink from the chance that deeper changes, some of them even democratic, might result from the conflict; and to these leading spirits there adhered throughout the community those Puritans and others whose sufferings or whose reasonings during the late Reign of Thorough and of Laud had carried them in advance of the rest in political theory. So it had been from the beginning of the war; but in 1644, as Mr. Bruce also points out, not only had this natural distribution of the Parliamentarians into the moderate or cautious party and the party of energy and movement become more obvious, but it had identified itself in great measure with that ecclesiastical division of the Parliamentarians into PRESBYTERIANS and INDEPENDENTS which had meanwhile occurred. The party of moderation and peace was now in the main the Presbyterian party, satisfied with that solution of the Church-question which was provided by the strict Presbyterian settlement recommended by the Westminster Assembly and as good as adopted by Parliament, and chiefly anxious now that the King should be brought to terms including the acceptance of that settlement. The party of movement, on the other hand, was now the Independent party, dissatisfied with the proposed settlement in itself, but, above all, resolute, since such a settlement appeared inevitable, that it should be accompanied by a sufficient toleration enactment, or guarantees for liberty of conscience, in behalf of non-Presbyterians. This question of liberty of conscience, indeed, had become practically the all-important one within the Parliamentarian ranks. For now, in addition to the PRESBYTERIANS and the INDEPENDENTS proper, one heard much of THE SECTS, *i.e.* of a vast miscellany of persons diffused through English society, who, though most of them were Independents too in the sense of holding by the principle of the "independency" of particular congregations of Christians, were yet distinguishable from the milder Independents of the Westminster Assembly by the fact that they had branched off into varieties and irregularities of religious belief which those divines did not profess to countenance. These sects were, as Mr. Bruce says, partly the product of the immediate ferment of the time, following on the break-up of Laud's rule and the abolition of Episcopacy; but they were partly also re-appearances of sects native in England since the Reformation, and which, though apparently suppressed by the rigour against Separatists through the reigns of Elizabeth, James, and Charles, had left remnants and seeds. *Brownists, Anabaptists, Antinomians, Seekers, Socinians,* &c., &c., were the names in all men's mouths, descriptive of the different classes of this religious medley, attached to the Independents. The existence of such sectaries, their rapid multiplication, and their growing boldness in venting their "heresies and blasphemies," were pointed to by the Presbyterians as proofs of the dangerous tendency of the principle of Church-independency; and the more orthodox Independents were tauntingly asked whether they were not ashamed of such a rag-tail of adherents, and whether they would extend the benefits of liberty of conscience to *them*. The Independents, on the whole, were obliged to say they would, though some of them did so reluctantly, and most of them still with the admission that, when religious error went beyond certain limits, it might lawfully be checked. More and more, therefore, "Presbytery and No Toleration" became the watchword of that great majority of the Parliamentarians which formed the moderate party, while the more extreme or revolutionary Puritanism, which wanted to throw increased energy into the war, took to itself more and more the name of Independency, and even passed beyond ordinary Independency into Anabaptism,

Antinomianism, Brownism, and other forms of sectarian opinion.—
D.M.]

Such opinions made easy way in the Army, especially in that part of it which was under the command of Cromwell, who possessed the faculty of imbuing other persons with his own opinions. His scheme of military reform was based upon the employment as soldiers of men in whom devotion to the public cause should act as a counterpoise to feelings of chivalry and loyalty. Such men were necessarily persons of intelligence, and, when Cromwell had the power of selection, men of religion, already imbued with the leading opinions and ready to put faith in the judgment of their commander. But, with the exception of the incident with Major-General Crawford, we have no information upon the subject, nor any indication of difference of opinion between Cromwell and the Earl of Manchester, until after the Battle of Marston Moor, from which time our narrative must become more minute.

[Mr. Bruce's manuscript now passes at once to the Battle of Marston Moor, skipping three months. It is vital to the story, however, that there should be some farther mention of the phenomenon upon which he has been touching, viz. the spread of Independency and Sectarianism in the Parliamentarian army, and especially in Cromwell's part of it, and also that some of the incidents of those three months should be noted.

Independency and Sectarianism had acquired gradually such strength in the various armies of Parliament that at length the Presbyterians of the two Houses and the Westminster Assembly had taken alarm. On the 2nd of April, 1644, the Scottish Baillie, then in London as a Commissioner to the Assembly, expressly noting the fact that the Army contained many Independents, adds that "sundry officers and soldiers" of that way of thinking had gone beyond it into " Antinomianism and Anabaptism."[a] On the 26th of the same month he again writes, " The Independents have so managed their affairs that of the officers and sojours in Man-

[a] Baillie, ii. 146.—D.M.

chester's army, certainly also in the General's (Essex's), and, as I hear, in Waller's likewise, more than the two parts (two-thirds) are for them, and these of the far most resolute and confident men for the Parliament party."ᵃ This, as Baillie soon came to know, was a great exaggeration at that time as regards Essex's and Waller's armies; but it was substantially true as regards Manchester's. One guesses, indeed, that Baillie had in his mind the recent affair of the Anabaptist Colonel Packer, in which his countryman, Major-General Crawford, had come so memorably into collision with Cromwell. At all events, Baillie and all the Presbyterians had their eyes fastened by this time on Manchester's army of the Associated Eastern Counties, as that most impregnated with Independency and other dangerous forms of opinion, and had learnt to associate the fact with Cromwell's hitherto all-powerful influence in that army. " Colonel Cromwell, the great Independent," is already Baillie's name for him. It was perfectly true in every sense. Although Cromwell, like other English Puritans, had sympathised with the Scots in their national struggle for Presbyterianism, although he had even inquired into the principles of Scottish Presbytery with a view to judge of its fitness for England, although he had signed the Solemn League and Covenant—pledging England and Scotland to a union in Church Reform—his reasonings had led him to a decided preference for the views of the Congregationalists. With them, he would have avoided, if possible, the importation of the exact Scottish Church-system into England; and, with them, he was resolute that, if it should be imported, it should be tempered to English ideas with a large, if not an unbounded, liberty of dissent. In his management of Manchester's army, and especially in his selection of officers under him, he had acted according to his own nature, his main principle being to choose men that "feared God and had a spirit for the business." Presbyterians were by no means to be rejected, if otherwise suitable; but naturally Independents were his favourites, and other such men as,

ᵃ Baillie, ii. 170.—D.M.

agreeing in essentials, would be easy and tolerant with each other in smaller differences. Neither now nor at any future time in Cromwell's life could observers assign him certainly to any one sect in particular, though the fervid sects, such as Anabaptists, Antinomians, and Seekers, seemed more congenial to him than the cooler and more sceptical sects that had also begun to be heard of: he was simply "the great Independent," looked up to by all the sects, and uniting them all on the common ground of liberty of conscience. Quietly and gradually, Manchester having let him have his own way, he had "packed" Manchester's army, it was now said, with religionists of his own type or of types as questionable; and that this was true to some extent appears from the fact that among the officers of that army at our present date one can count Pickering, Whalley, the two Lilburnes, Fleetwood, Montague, Hammond, Rainsborough, Harrison, and others, some of them very young men, all ardent disciples of Cromwell already, and to be known as more or less faithful to him in coming years. It was into this "happy family" that the precisian and Presbyterian Major-General Crawford had stepped; and we have seen the first consequence.

The difference between Lieutenant-General Cromwell and Major-General Crawford over the affair of the Anabaptist colonel was still a matter of rankling in Manchester's army when, late in April 1644, active military operations recommenced. Again Essex made objections to the encroachments on his authority caused by the existence of so many armies under separate commands, and by the regulation of all by the Derby House Committee of both Kingdoms; but again he was overruled and pacified.ᵃ The Derby House Committee was renewed; and there were still, as before, to be five sectional armies for the

---

ᵃ I find among Mr. Bruce's papers of jottings extracts from the Lords and Commons Journals of April and May 1644 referring more particularly to Essex's remonstrances about the independent power given to the Earl of Manchester. This is one more proof of Mr Bruce's industry in collecting materials for enlarging and completing his Preface.—D.M.

HISTORICAL PREFACE.   xli

Parliament—Essex's own and Waller's of 10,000 men each for the midlands and south, that of the Fairfaxes and the auxiliary army of the Scots for the north, and Manchester's for the eastern counties. For this last army, through the whole of May, there was a good deal of renewed special work in Nottinghamshire and Lincolnshire, including the siege and capture of Lincoln itself;[a] and there is proof that even during that month Crawford found additional reason for rancour against Cromwell.[b] But another and more extraordinary piece of service for Manchester's army was at hand. The army of the Fairfaxes and the Scottish auxiliary army had brought matters to such a pass in the north that the siege of York was now the great enterprise in that region; and, Manchester's army having crossed the Humber to assist in this enterprise, the three armies, or rather portions of them, to the number of about 25,000 men in all, beleaguered York all through June, skirmishing and pushing on the attacks. Here again, according to Crawford's account (Narrative, p. 60), he had ample opportunity of knowing that Cromwell was taking the entire control of Manchester's army, and especially of the Horse, into his own hands, and using his Lieutenant-Generalship, with the help of his "creatures," for the discredit of Manchester and the furtherance of the sectarian interest. Crawford himself, we have to infer, was doing his best to counteract this Cromwellian influence, and was gathering round him those Presbyterian officers whom Cromwell had aggrieved or who longed to escape from his domination. Unfortunately, a feat of Crawford's at the siege of York, of which we do not hear from himself, was not of a nature to enhance his reputation in rivalry with Cromwell even among his fellow-Presbyterians. On the 16th of June, "hoping to

[a] Rushworth, v. 620-622.—D.M.
[b] See Crawford's own *ex parte* "narrative" in the Documents in this volume (pp. 59-60); and connect therewith this passage in Baillie of date May 19th, 1644: "*We are advertised* that much more than the most part of my Lord Manchester's army are reduced to Independency, and very many of them have added either Anabaptism or Antinomianism, or both."—Baillie, ii. 185.—D.M.

CAMD. SOC.   *g*

take the city himself," he sprang a mine without orders and dashed in through the breach so made, with the result of a repulse and the loss of 300 men.[a] Crawford's "foolish rashness" and "great vanity" in this business were confessed even by his countryman Baillie in London,[b] and he seems to have collapsed for the rest of the siege. On the 1st of July, however, when the Marquis of Newcastle could defend York no longer, and was on the point of giving it up, the approach of Rupert for his relief, after a northward march distinguished by various successes, obliged the besiegers to desist, and try the issue in a great pitched battle in the vicinity. Thus came about the BATTLE OF MARSTON MOOR, the first supremely momentous battle of the Civil War.—D.M.]

That great battle was fought on Tuesday the 2nd July, 1644, almost under the walls of York. It was won by the division of the Parliamentary army under the command of the Earl of Manchester and Cromwell, in combination with the forces of Yorkshire under Lord Fairfax and his son Sir Thomas, and those of the Scots under the Earl of Leven and Generals [Baillie and] Leslie. The bloody contest continued from seven o'clock in the evening until ten o'clock, in the moon-lit twilight of a mid-summer night. It was fought amidst much confusion, and the contemporary accounts which have descended to us partake of the doubts and inexactness of the original writers.[e] Even now historians are not agreed as to the number or the disposition of the forces engaged on either side. But no one doubts as to the results. Rupert gathered up the fragments of his broken army and hurried off through Lancashire into Shropshire to recruit. The Marquis of Newcastle and General King forsook their men and their cause, and made their way to

[a] Rushworth, v. 631.—D.M.
[b] See letter of Baillie of date June 1644, ii. 195.—D.M.
[e] The best account we have is that of Mr. Sandford in his *Studies and Illustrations of the Great Rebellion*, 8vo. 1858, a most valuable book. [See a later paper on the subject, entitled "A Visit to Marston Moor," by the late Mr. Herman Merivale, in *Macmillan's Magazine* for July 1862.—D.M.]

Scarborough and thence into Holland [with a large following of Royalists of rank]. York surrendered on the 20th July.

[Mixed up with the rejoicings among the Parliamentarians all through England, and especially in London, over the grand victory of Marston Moor, was the question which part of the combined army and which of the generals concerned were chiefly entitled to the credit. What was substantially the truth seems to have reached London at once, viz., that none of the three generals-in-chief could claim any of the merit, all three having been somehow carried off the field in flight, and that the battle had been won by Cromwell at the head of Manchester's horse, ably seconded by Major-General David Leslie at the head of a few Scottish troops. But for some time there were fluctuations of rumour on the subject, caused by the reluctance of the Presbyterians to admit that the honours of the day had been won by "the great Independent" and his sectarian Ironsides, and especially by the anger of the Scots at the small allowance of praise accorded in the London journals to the Scottish auxiliary army. This is curiously illustrated in Baillie's letters. "The Independents sent up one quickly to assure that all the glory of that night was theirs, that they and their General Cromwell had done it all their alone," he writes on the 12th of July, adding that Captain Stuart, a Scot, had since arrived to " show the vanity and falsehood of their disgraceful relation," and to tell that David Leslie had really begun the victory, and how much of the burden of the battle besides had been borne by the Scottish Foot under Lieutenant-General Baillie.[a] Again, on the 16th, writing to his friend Robert Blair, then one of the chaplains in the Scottish auxiliary army, he says :—

We were both grieved and angry that your Independents there should have sent up Major Harrison to trumpet over all the city their own praises to our prejudice, making all believe that Cromwell alone, with his unspeakably valorous regiments, had done all that service—that the

[a] Baillie, ii. 203-204.— D.M.

most of *us* [the Scots] fled, and who stayed they fought so and so as it might be. We were much vexed with these reports, against which you were not pleased, any of you, to instruct us with any answer till Lindsay's letters came at last and Captain Stuart with his colours. Then we sent abroad *our* printed relations, and could lift up our face. But within three days Mr. Ashe's relation was also printed, who gives *us* many good words, but gives much more to Cromwell than we are informed is his due. Let good Mr. Ashe [Manchester's army-chaplain and a Presbyterian] know what is the use that generally here is made of his relations, much, I know, beside his intention: even this in plain terms, The Independents have done so brave service, yea they are so strong and considerable a party, that they must not only be tolerate, but in nothing grieved.[a]

Again, on the 23rd, to another correspondent,

Our Independents [of the Westminster Assembly] continues and increases in their obstinacy. Much is added to their pride and hopes by their service at the Battle of York, albeit much of their valour is grounded on very false lies, prejudicial to God, the author, and to *us* [Scots], the true instrument of that day's honour.[b]

Finally, as late as August 10, speaking of the Independents generally, Baillie writes:—

The men are exceeding active in their own way; they strive to advance Cromwell for their head. They ascribe to him the victory of York, but most unjustly; for Humbie [Sir Adam Hepburn, Laird of Humbie, Commissary-General of the Scottish auxiliary army] assures us that Prince Rupert's first charge falling on him did humble him so that, if David Leslie had not supported them, he had fled. Sheldon Crawford, who had a regiment of dragoons in that wing, upon his oath assured me that at the beginning of the fight Cromwell got a little wound in the craig [neck], which made him retire, so that he was not so much as present at the service, but his troopers were led on by David Leslie.[c]

[a] Baillie, ii. 208-209.—D.M. [b] Ibid. 211.—D.M. [c] Ibid. 218.—D.M.

The "Sheldon Crawford" here mentioned is not the Major-General Crawford of Manchester's army, with whom we have chiefly to do, but William Crawford, of Nether Sheldon in Ayrshire, a lieutenant-colonel of dragoons in the Scottish auxiliary army. He, too, had the Scottish and Presbyterian antipathy to Cromwell; and, having run up to London after Marston Moor, he had talked of Cromwell very much as his namesake the major-general would have done.[a] In spite of all, Cromwell emerged more and more clearly in public opinion as the true hero of Marston Moor; and Baillie and the Scots had to console themselves as well as they could with the hypothesis that this was owing to the systematic puffing of him by the Independents and their command of the London press for the purpose. Meanwhile, York having been taken, the necessary combination of the three Parliamentary armies which had led to such important results had been judged no longer necessary or convenient, and they were about to part company. Mr. Bruce proceeds to describe the circumstances of the separation, and to follow Manchester's army on *its* particular route southwards again. —D.M.]

The fall of the northern capital and the flight of Prince Rupert to the southward substantially brought the whole of the kingdom beyond the Humber under the dominion of the Parliament. There remained indeed a few fortified places, principally houses scattered about Yorkshire, but they were comparatively unimportant; Scarborough and Newcastle, the latter a great centre of commerce and communication, were the chief towns on the eastern coast over which the royal standard still waved.

The destruction of the Marquis of Newcastle's army and the reduction of Yorkshire, the objects which had brought the armies

---

[a] Rushworth, v. 605, and note by Mr. David Laing to Baillie, ii. 218. See note in this Preface, *ante*, p. xxii. It is very natural to confound this "Sheldon Crawford" with "Major-General Crawford," the rather as the major-general afterwards made accusations against Cromwell like those in the text, or worse. Godwin and other writers have made the mistake.—D.M.

of Manchester, Fairfax, and the Scots together, having been accomplished, it rested with the central authority—the Committee of Both Kingdoms—to direct their subsequent movements by fresh instructions. Manchester did not wait long for them. No endeavour had been made to pursue Prince Rupert, although the Committee had urged that course in letters addressed to the three generals on the 9th and 19th July;[a] but, two days after the surrender of York, Manchester apprised the Committee that the great necessities of his army, and those of the Scots, had induced them to separate. He wrote from Ferrybridge, on his way to Doncaster; the Scots were at Leeds and Wakefield; whilst Fairfax had taken possession of York. Manchester described his men as falling sick daily "through want of clothes and other necessaries;" he prayed they might be preserved from pestilence. At Doncaster he should await the commands of the Committee.[b]

On the 27th July he announced that, having summoned Tickhill Castle, [in Yorkshire, but on the very border of Nottinghamshire] and sent into the town 300 dragoons, the garrison had surrendered. "I have taken" he remarked, "some 120 arms, some 80 horse, and have given liberty to the gentlemen to go unto their several dwellings, because they referred themselves very much to my disposal."[c]

In the meantime the Committee had received from Sir Adam Hepburn and Mr. Hatcher, messengers despatched from the armies of the Scots and Manchester, more precise information of their condition. They had also learnt that Prince Rupert, "with the assistance of the Earl of Derby," who was "very active and of great power," was [busily] recruiting "in Lancashire." Having possession of Liverpool, it was anticipated that succours would come to him out of Ireland, and that in a short time he would be in condition to make another of his dashing forays, the direction of which it was difficult to foresee, and perhaps even to fight another battle of

[a] Letter Book of the Committee of Both Kingdoms under those dates.
[b] Letters received by the Committee 22nd July, 1644.
[c] Ibid. 27th July, 1644.

Marston Moor. The Committee, having " taken these things into serious debate, at which Sir Adam Hepburn and Mr. Hatcher were present," reiterated their desire that the three lords would make some endeavour to avert such a calamity. They allowed that there might be difficulties in the march of the whole army; they agreed that the enemy could not " be pursued through difficult passages, nor with speed, by a great body with artillery and carriages," [a] and that " the following a light, flying enemy " would harass out and break an army, whereof there " had been too much experience;" but they still urged co-operation with the forces of Lancashire and those parts, and the despatch of such a body of auxiliaries as, in conjunction with the local forces, " might be able to go up to the Prince and fight with him." " What ways to march, what number, and with what forces," the Committee concluded, " you who are upon the place can best judge, to whom we leave it." [b]

Manchester's answer, which is dated from Blyth [in Nottinghamshire, a few miles south of Tickhill] on the 1st August, 1644, announced that the generals and other chief officers of the three armies had held a consultation " what was fittest to be done upon the letter of the Committee." They found that the information concerning Prince Rupert's being in Lancashire could not be relied upon, for that he and all his best horse had passed over into Cheshire at Haleford, and that his "dragooners" [c] and such remainder of foot as he had were " daily boated over from Liverpool." " The rest of his horse under the command of Goring, together with some foot under Colonel Clavering and the Earl of Montrose, are marched towards Cumberland and Westmoreland, so as Lancashire have only some petty garrisons left, which the forces in the county, if well employed, may easily master." Upon this state of things, as if Lancashire, and not Rupert, had been the object of solicitude with

[a] *i.e.* with baggage or things to be carried; the same sense in which the word is used in the authorised translation of Acts [xxi. 15].
[b] Letter Book of the Committee under the date.
[c] Dragoons.

the Committee, the consulting officers had determined "thus" to divide their forces: "that I," remarks the Earl, "should march southward, and that the Scots . . . should march for the security of those northern counties, and to intend the taking in of Newcastle." In pursuance of this resolution Manchester announced his intention to be at Lincoln by Saturday night, the 4th August, when he should devote himself to recruiting and refreshing his troops, and would attend the commands of the Committee which way they would have him to march and what they would have him to do. He concludes with some remarks upon his difficulties in recruiting, and upon a rumour that his troops were " really and fully paid," which of course was not at all true ; but in spite of every obstacle he protested his readiness, with that force he had, and which yet he hoped might do the Committee some service, to obey their orders.[a] In a postscript the amiable Earl added: " Since my coming to Blyth I hear there is two regiments of horse come to Newark from Prince Rupert, with the assurance that the Prince will send some foot thither with all speed, but I hope neither his horse or foot shall do any hurt to that county. I shall make the more haste into it."

The postscript illustrates not only the comparative activity of the Prince and the Earl, but confirms the Earl's letter in exhibiting his affection for "county" considerations in the management of the war. Newark was one of the most important places in that part of England. It belonged territorially to the Queen, and the inhabitants were full of loyalty to the sovereign lady of the manor. Besides which, it locally commanded the communications between Lincolnshire, and consequently between the eastern counties, and York. It had been strongly garrisoned by the Marquis of Newcastle, and, at the beginning of this year, had been besieged by the Parliamentarians under Sir John Meldrum. It was reduced to the greatest straits, but Rupert by a masterly march from Shrewsbury came, just in time, to their relief. He took the besiegers by surprise. Without

[a] Letter Book of Letters received by the Committee under date.

waiting for his foot, he dashed in upon the besiegers with his cavalry. They took refuge in a place called the Spittle, which they had fortified. Besieged in their turn, and without provisions, they soon surrendered upon easy terms, but their losses in the field were heavy, and they relinquished all their artillery, their arms, and ammunition. The Earl, it will be observed, did not contemplate resuming the siege, but, in the interest of the country, expressed in a jaunty way his kind-hearted desire and intention to restrain the loyalist foragers.

Pursuing his career of easy but by no means unprofitable victories, the Earl advanced from Tickhill and Blyth to Lincoln, paying a triumphant and of course a courteous visit on his way to Welbeck, the magnificent seat of his vanquished opponent, the Marquis of Newcastle. In his haste to avoid the sneers of Oxford on his defeat at Marston, the Marquis had left his family in the seclusion of that stately home, still rich with the recollections of the vain-glorious ceremonials which had distinguished it on past visits of the Marquis's royal master.[a] The story of the Earl's courteous reception by the deserted inmates and his own polite returns had best be told in his own words [from Lincoln, Aug. 6]:—

In my march from York towards Lincoln I was earnestly intreated by divers in those parts of Yorkshire about Sheffield, that I would consider of the great spoil that the garrison in Sheffield did unto the places near adjoining, and likewise of the consequence of the place in regard of the great commodity of iron wares that were vented there. I was further moved by the Committees and gentlemen of Nottingham for the reducing of the garrison in Welbeck to the obedience of Parliament, because it was a great annoyance to those parts; whereupon I resolved to go myself with a great part of my forces to Welbeck, and to send General-Major Crawford with the rest unto Sheffield. Upon my coming near

---

[a] Perhaps the most famous of these was Charles's visit to Welbeck on his way to Scotland in the summer of 1633 for his coronation there. Part of the entertainment consisted in the performance of *Love's Welcome*, a masque by Ben Jonson, written for the occasion.—D.M.

Welbeck, I sent in a summons to the place, and they, with great civility, sent to parley with me. And the next day, being Friday, they rendered the House unto me upon composition. I was willing to give them the larger terms, because I was not in a condition to besiege a place so well fortified as that was, and therefore I gave the officers and soldiers liberty to march with all their arms, colours flying, and other punctilios of war. But, when I came to take possession of the house, most of all the soldiers came unto me to lay down their arms, and would not carry them, but desired tickets of me to go to their own homes, the which I granted them; so as I had 350 muskets in the house, fifty horse arms, eleven pieces of cannon great and small, whereof one the Governor had liberty to carry away. I had likewise twenty barrels of powder and a ton of match. The house I preserved entire, and have put a garrison into it of Nottinghamshire men, until I know your Lordships' resolution whether you will have it slighted or not. The place is very regularly fortified, and the Marquis of Newcastle's daughters, and the rest of his children and family, are in it, unto whom I have engaged myself for their quiet abode there, and to intercede to the Parliament for a complete maintenance for them. In the which I shall beseech your Lordships that they may have your favour and furtherance. I am now myself come to Lincoln, and those forces that were with me I have quartered about Gainsborough and those places, that I may give them some refreshing after the great hardship they have endured.

He concludes with some comments upon a recent ordinance of Parliament[a] for putting the Associated Counties, of which he was the military head, "into a posture of defence," by raising fresh forces of horse and foot, and giving the persons listed upon that service the power to propound and nominate their own colonels and other officers, subject to the approval of the lord-lieutenants.[b] The Earl suspected, or felt inclined to believe, that these new arrangements were inconsistent with his authority, and desired to know what were the intentions of the Committee:—

[a] Dated 3rd July, 1644.   [b] Husband, 516.

If your Lordships please to have me to deliver over the remainder of this force I now have into the hands of those colonels and captains that are to be chosen to give a supply to that army that is now to be raised, I shall very readily obey your order; if your Lordships' intentions be to dispose of these forces otherwise, I shall with all care observe your commands.[a]

In all these arrangements of the Earl there was no doubt much that was agreeable to the Committee. Tickhill and Welbeck were thorns in the sides of the people dwelling within the Parliamentary line. Their garrisons lived by the plunder of their Roundhead neighbours; or, if kept in order by forces stationed in neighbouring towns, such forces could have been far better employed elsewhere, besides that such fortified places hindered all free communication across the country. But all these minor victories of the heroes of Marston Moor were dimmed in the appreciation of the Committee by the cloud which hung over the movements of Prince Rupert. The suddenness and violence of his onslaughts had taught them the necessity of continual watchfulness and preparedness. For the third time, writing to the Earl on the date of his letter to them, they reiterate their directions in unmistakeable language:—

We have taken into consideration the necessity of hindering the recruits of Prince Rupert, and wholly to break his army, if it be possible. And to that end we desire you to gather what force you can get together forthwith. And with them (together with the forces of Nottinghamshire, Derbyshire, and Lancashire, as also those of Sir William Brereton and Sir Thomas Middleton, to all of which we have written to that purpose, and to receive your orders) to march toward Prince Rupert and attend his motions, and follow him which way soever he shall go, and to take all advantages against him that shall be offered.

They add that they have taken measures to procure his soldiers their pay, which shall be sent to him wherever he may be, and that,

[a] Book of Letters received by the Committee, under date of 6th August, 1644. [See Documents, pp. 5, 7.]

us for the New Ordinance on which he had commented, it would be rather to his advantage than the contrary in procuring recruits.[a] By subsequent letters of the 7th and the 9th they intimate to him that the House of Commons had ordered that 1800 foot of the troops levied under the New Ordinance should be sent to him as recruits, but that in selecting that number he was to take no more than necessity required out of Essex, because an entire formed regiment of 1000 men was to be raised by that county.

Orders so peremptory came most unseasonably upon the kind and considerate Earl. They overturned all his own schemes for refreshing his victorious Marston men. To attend Prince Rupert's motions and follow him which way soever he should go was "so large a commission, and work so difficult, considering the weak condition of his forces with their indispositions and infections," that he called together such of his chief officers as were with him at the time to consult what he was to do. The result was a paper of "considerations," or rather objections, which he transmitted from Lincoln on the 10th of August. It does not appear who were the objectors. Their objections were the merest common-place excuses of unwillingness. It could not be expected that they should force Prince Rupert to a second engagement that summer, nor, considering his defensible position at Chester, was it likely that they could force him to "go away." If he did and they were to follow him through Wales, or wherever they went, it would ruin their own army. Besieging Chester was out of the question; it would be as great a work as that which they had just accomplished at York. All they could do would be to lie near Chester and hinder the Prince from receiving any accession of force, which would necessarily keep them there all the winter. Then, how were they to secure their supplies and recruits, and the back pay they were to receive, which would have to pass under the walls of Belvoir, Newark, Bolsover, and Tidbury and other garrisons of the enemies? Those four fortified places ought first to be taken or blocked up, and the Earl's forces were

[a] Book of Letters sent under date of 6th August, 1644. [Documents, pp. 4-5.]

insufficient for any thing of the kind, his foot, "sick and sound," not amounting to more than 6,000 men. Finally, it was urged that the Association of the Eastern Counties, by which Lord Manchester's forces were raised and should be paid, had been already much discontented at their withdrawal into the north, [and] would, if they were now to draw off so far westward, have just cause to withdraw from their recruiting or maintenance, and seek some other body and head to protect them.[a]

A representation which trenched so close upon insubordination must have tried the temper of the Committee; but it was their cue, in the confused and precarious condition of public affairs, not to try conclusions with anyone. They complimented the Earl on his successes at Welbeck, and afterwards at Sheffield, where Major-General Crawford was successful; they alleged that the state of Prince Rupert's army being other than they conceived, many of his forces having marched northward, and a consideration of the reasons which the Earl had inclosed to them, had caused them to alter their resolutions. They now desired him merely to send such a party as he should think fit to join with the forces to be sent from Nottinghamshire, Derbyshire, ...

* * * * * *

CONTINUATION.

[At this point, August 14, 1644, Mr. Bruce's fragments of his Preface abruptly stop. It was evidently his purpose to narrate the history of Manchester's campaign, in the same style, partly by continued abstract of the correspondence between Manchester and the Derby House Committee, but with light from other sources, on to the second battle of Newbury, October 27, 1644, when the long-smouldering quarrel between Manchester and Cromwell publicly exploded into flame, and then to trace the quarrel itself through the two Houses in the subsequent months, till, in the beginning of

[a] [Documents of Manchester's Correspondence, pp. 8-12.]

1645, it was hushed up in a total recast of the whole army-system of the Parliament, devised or approved by Cromwell, and rendering the further prosecution of his quarrel with Manchester quite unnecessary. The following may pass as a substitute for what might have come from Mr. Bruce's pen.—D.M.]

The inactivity of Manchester, his evasion of work recommended to him or even enjoined upon him, his indisposition to leave his own district of the Associated Counties, continue obvious in the correspondence between him and the Derby House Committee. He had arrived at Lincoln on the 4th of August, and he was still there and idle on the 4th of September, having in the first place managed to decline the expedition into Cheshire in pursuit of Rupert by pleading that Newark and other garrisons of the enemy near Lincoln ought first to be dealt with, and having in the next place avoided all effort about those garrisons. One can see, even through the polite phraseology of the letters of the Derby House Committee, that there was considerable dissatisfaction at headquarters with this state of matters, the Presbyterian members of that Committee, such as the Scottish Lord Maitland, evidently now agreeing with the Independent members, such as Viscount Saye and Sele, in the opinion that the great success of Marston Moor ought to have been more vigorously followed up.

But what of Manchester's own army, and especially of those Ironsides in it, Cromwell's horse, who were the heroes of Marston Moor? That Manchester's policy of idleness had the sanction of a considerable number of his officers is to be inferred from the fact that he had been able to send from Lincoln to the Derby House Committee on the 10th of August a paper of reasons against the Cheshire expedition, purporting to be the result of a consultation with such of his chief officers as were then about him; but that Cromwell and his adherents were dissatisfied there is abundant proof. They were more than dissatisfied; they were vehemently roused.

Among Cromwell's preserved letters as published by Mr. Carlyle there are but two belonging to this period, one dated from Lincoln, Sept. 1, the other from Sleaford, somewhat south of Lincoln, Sept. 5 or 6. The latter, which is addressed to his brother-in-law Colonel Valentine Walton, then in London, contains this passage:—

We have some amongst us much slow in action; if we could all intend our own ends less and our ease too, our business in this army would go on wheels for expedition. But, because some of us are enemies to rapine and other wickednesses, we are said to be "factious," to "seek to maintain our opinions in religion by force,"—which we detest and abhor. I profess I could never satisfy myself of the justness of this War, but from the authority of the Parliament to maintain itself in its rights; and in this Cause I hope to approve myself an honest man and single-hearted. Pardon me that I am thus troublesome. I write but seldom : it gives me a little ease to pour my mind, in the midst of calumnies, into the bosom of a friend.[a]

These words, vague in their mournfulness, receive adequate illustration for the first time in the two documents published in the present volume under the titles *Cromwell's Narrative* and *Narrative of the Earl of Manchester's Campaign*, which last is in fact *Crawford's Narrative*. From Cromwell himself we now learn, in the first of these documents, the exact causes of that mood of sorrow which he communicated to Colonel Walton. From Marston Moor to the date at which he wrote, the whole conduct of Manchester's army had been, in his opinion, a tissue of mismanagement. Newark might have been taken or blockaded; there might have been the march after Rupert; at the very least a body of horse might have been sent for service in Cheshire; even within the range to which the Earl had confined himself hundreds of useful things might have been done, besides the taking of Tickhill Castle and Welbeck House—which petty exploits themselves had actually been forced on the Earl and done against his will! The army had been quar-

[a] Carlyle's *Cromwell*, i. 157, ed. 1857.

tered upon the friends of Parliament precisely in those parts of the eastern region where there was nothing to do, leaving other parts free for the enemy to range in! Only one Council of War had been called by the Earl since he left York! Considering all this, Cromwell had come reluctantly in his own mind to one conclusion —to wit, that the Earl's fault was not improvidence only, but an incorrigible " backwardness to all action," caused by " some principle of unwillingness " to see the King brought " too low."

Now, though Cromwell had not publicly expressed his opinion in this degree of strength at the date we have reached, he had certainly expressed the substance of it in such ways that the Earl could not remain ignorant of the fact that he had lost the confidence of his Lieutenant-General. One infers also that Cromwell had taken means to convey his impressions to the Derby House Committee and other authorities in London; and it is worth noting, in this connection, that Cromwell's disciple, young Fleetwood, had been in London in August, and was the bearer of some of the Committee's letters of that month back to the Earl at Lincoln. Clearly the relations between the commander-in-chief of the Eastern Army and his lieutenant-general were now those of schism,—Cromwell speaking out his mind frankly whenever he could; and the Earl resenting his advices, and treating him with as much coolness as was permissible towards a man of such antecedents, who could make himself so terrible when he chose. Even convenient to the Earl might now be those Presbyterian alarms about Cromwell's Independency, and his sympathies with Anabaptism and other heresies, which in the earlier days of their co-operation had counted for so little. Cries about Cromwell's sectarian factiousness, and his forcing of his own religious opinions into the army by ejecting orthodox men from posts and putting sectarians into them, were doubtless now encouraged among the Earl's partisans, and seem to have been the " calumnies " of which Cromwell speaks in his letter to his brother-in-law. No mention is made in Cromwell's narrative of Major-General Crawford's doings at this time, because, when the narrative was written, it was unnecessary to revert to *him*; but that Crawford had a conspicuous part in the schism is only what might have been expected, and is expressly vouched by himself. Crawford, it is true, had been out of Lincolnshire during the greater part of August, employed, with 1,200 foot and a regiment of horse, in that special service of the taking of Sheffield Castle for which he had been detached, and to which he had added the capture of Bolsover Castle and one or two other houses in Derbyshire.[a] But, both during his absence and after his return to the main army in Lincolnshire in the end of August, he gives us to understand, Cromwell had been at his old tricks, " taking all the praise to himself of other men's actions " (at Marston Moor and elsewhere), promoting actual " mutiny," screening and protecting men of his own " godly " sort in any delinquency, and labouring, with his " juncto," to bring good officers into discredit. Especially had Crawford been the object of his enmity. " All this time," he says, in his peculiarly clotted grammar, " the said Cromwell endeavoured to work Major-General's Crawford's ruin by dissuading the Earl of Manchester's army not to obey him, and, giving his charge away to others, making them to do the duty, did in the most notorious manner traduce and calumniate the said Crawford, to make him odious to the army and to discontent him, that so he the said Cromwell the better might advance his wicked ends, uttering many speeches highly to his disadvantage and utter ruin, and for drawing of factions in the army, which highly distracted the public good in Lincoln." The regiments of Colonels Pickering and Montague are mentioned as chief among those that, on Cromwell's instigation, " absolutely refused orders from Major-General Crawford." The correct interpretation of all this is not difficult. Cromwell did regard the introduction of Crawford into Manchester's army as the original cause of the mischief, and he was willing for the time to direct his full fury against *him* rather than against the Earl, in the

[a] Rushworth, v. 642-645.

hope perhaps that, if Crawford were removed, the Earl might resume his better mind, and be induced to a more active strategy.[a]

At last, willingly or unwillingly, the Earl *was* on the move. On the 5th of September, the day of Cromwell's letter to Walton from Sleaford in Lincolnshire, the Earl was at Bourne, still farther south in the same county, having left Lincoln on the previous day; and thence he advanced to Huntingdon, where he was on the 8th. He was still within his favourite region of the Association, but that he was in motion at all portended something. In fact he had yielded at last so far to repeated missives from Derby House, informing him that the services of his army were urgently required in the west, and appointing Abingdon on the borders of Berks and Oxfordshire as his rendezvous.

The reasons were most serious. Since Marston Moor had secured the north for the Parliament, the main stress of the war had been in the Midlands and south-west, where Essex and Waller were the two Parliamentary generals. After co-operating for some time against the King in the Midlands, these two generals had separated in June 1644, Essex persisting in undertaking that expedition against Prince Maurice and his Royalists in the south-west which the Parliament had designed for Waller, and Waller remaining in the Midlands. A kind of defeat sustained by Waller, on the Oxfordshire border, on the 29th of June (three days before Marston Moor), had enabled the King to follow Essex into the south-west, with the intention of joining Prince Maurice, and so crushing Essex by superior force. Essex, instead of turning back to fight the King, had been persuaded to push into Cornwall; in which extremely Royalist county, the King and Maurice having joined their armies, he found himself cooped up in the month of August in a most precarious condition. To send Waller for his relief with a newly equipped army was then the strenuous effort of the Parliament;

---

[a] The passages of Cromwell's narrative and of Crawford's more particularly founded on in this paragraph will be found at pp. 78-83 and pp. 60-62 of the appended Documents.

and, as Rupert was sure to move southwards to complicate matters, it was also a necessary part of their plan that Manchester's army should come out of its quarters in the Eastern Counties and follow Waller's route westward, or at least take his place in the Midlands. Hence the urgent missives to Manchester in Lincoln, and hence his march thence southwards, and his presence in Huntingdon on the 8th of September. By that time, however, Essex's fate in Cornwall had been decided. Before relief could reach him he had been obliged to make his own escape by sea to Plymouth on his way to London, leaving his horse under Sir William Balfour to cut their way eastward as they could, and his foot under Skippon to negotiate terms of surrender (Sept. 1). This news must have reached Manchester in Huntingdon; whence on the 8th of September he writes to the Derby House Committee, expressing his condolence over the sad event. "The Lord's arm," he adds, "is not shortened, though we be much weakened. I trust he will give us a happy recovery. I shall, with all the speed I can, march in observance of your former orders." Two notes to him from the Committee, dated Sept. 9 and Sept. 11, show that in their opinion their former orders were still to be obeyed. The King would now be on his return from Cornwall to Oxford, and the forces formerly destined for Essex's relief would now have to oppose the King in his return march. Let Manchester, therefore, still make westward for Abingdon with all possible expedition, and let him send the Committee advertisement of his marches as he proceeds!

From Sept. 11, the date of the Committee's last note, to Sept. 22, there is a gap in the correspondence between them and Manchester. The information as to what happened in this interval must be sought elsewhere.

The feud in Manchester's army and similar feuds in others had been greatly distressing Parliament and the Derby House Committee. "Concerning those differences which your Lordships take notice to be amongst some of this army," Manchester had written to the Committee in his letter from Huntingdon, " I hope your Lordships shall find that I shall take such care as, by the blessing of God, nothing of the public service shall be retarded." But the Committee were not content with private references to this subject. On the 10th of September they addressed a formal letter, signed by Viscount Saye and Sele and the Scottish Chancellor Lord Loudoun, to all "the principal commanders" of the armies, commenting on their jealousies, and imploring them to lay these aside and act cordially together for the common cause.[a] Within three days after that letter was written, Manchester, Cromwell, and Major-General Crawford, were all three in London on the business of the schism which had so long been distracting *their* particular army. The story is told most graphically by Baillie, and nothing more is necessary than to quote his account:—

The most of the officers in the General's [Essex's] and Waller's army, [writes Baillie on the 16th of September] has open and known quarrels. Manchester's army is more pitifully divided: it is like to divide us all incontinent. Manchester himself, a sweet meek man, permitted his Lieutenant-General Cromwell to guide all the army at his pleasure: the man is a very wise and active head, universally well beloved, as religious and stout; being a known Independent, the most of the sojours who loved new ways put themselves under his command. Our countryman Crawford was made General-Major of that army. This man, proving very stout and successful, got a great hand with Manchester, and with all the army that were not for sects. The other party, finding all their designs marred by him, set themselves by all means to have him out of the way, that, he being removed, they might frame the whole army to their devotion, and draw Manchester himself to them by persuasion, or else to weary him out of his charge, that Cromwell might be general. This has been the Independents' great plot by this army, to counterbalance us [the Scots], to overawe the Assembly and Parliament both to their ends. At this nick of time, while their service is necessary to oppose the King, they give in a challenge against Crawford: they require a Committee of War to remove him. Both the parties writes up here to

[a] See the Letter, Rushworth, v. 719, 720.

their friends the case: *at last Manchester, Cromwell, and Crawford, come up themselves.* Our labour to reconcile them was vain: Cromwell was peremptor; notwithstanding the kingdom's evident hazard, and the evident displeasure of our nation, yet, if Crawford were not cashiered, his Colonels would lay down their commissions. All of us, by my Lord Manchester's own testimony and the testimony of the ministers in the army, finds Crawford a very honest and valorous man, in nothing considerable guilty, only persecuted to make way to their designs on that army, and by it on the Parliament and kingdom; therefore all here of our friends resolves to see him get as little wrong as we may. What the end of this may be God knows.[a]

Baillie then notes another incident of Cromwell's visit to town as of surpassing importance:—

While Cromwell is here the House of Commons, without the least advertisement to any of us [the Scottish Commissioners in London], or of the Assembly, passes an order that the Grand Committee of both Houses, Assembly, and us, shall consider of the means to unite us [the Presbyterians] and the Independents; or, if that be found impossible, to see how they may be tolerate. This has much affected us.[b]

The gap in Manchester's Correspondence is now sufficiently accounted for. The Earl, his Lieutenant-General, and his Major-General, had hurriedly come to London, there to argue out their differences in person, before the Committee of the Two Kingdoms, or Committees of the Houses; and Cromwell had been so vehement against Crawford, and had so many Independents and others on his side, that the Scots and their Presbyterian friends had to exert themselves to the utmost in Crawford's behalf. But Cromwell had turned his brief visit to even larger account. Appearing in his place in the House of Commons, and advising with some of his friends there, he had suddenly, and without previous warning, got the House to pass what came to be called " The Accommodation

[a] Baillie, ii. 229-230.   [b] Ibid. 230.

Order," *i.e.* an order to a great Committee of the Lords and Commons, then in regular conference with the Scottish Commissioners and a Committee of the Westminster Assembly, to try to compose the differences between the Presbyterians and the Independents in the Assembly, and, if they failed in that, to devise some means for a moderate toleration of dissent under the Church system that might be established. The date of this order was Sept. 13. Cromwell himself was the real mover, though St. John and Vane carried it through the House, and St. John was responsible for the very cautious wording. "The great shot of Cromwell and Vane," says Baillie, " is to have a liberty for all religions, without any exceptions;" but St. John had thought it judicious not to frame the order so as to alarm the House by that implication. As it was, the order was a most disagreeable surprise to the Presbyterians. The Presbyterian system had not yet been carried completely through the Assembly itself, much less brought into Parliament; and here virtually was a Toleration Clause inserted by anticipation into the Bill for establishing Presbytery when it should come to be passed. Altogether, Cromwell's hasty visit to London in Sept. 1644 was to be a very memorable matter.

Manchester, Cromwell, and Crawford (not dismissed, after all), were again away at their posts in the army. On the 22nd of September the Earl was at Watford; and on the 27th he was still no farther west than Harefield on the borders of Bucks and Middlesex, but with Cromwell detached in advance of him. It is only necessary to read the letters that passed in this week between him and the Derby House Committee (*Correspondence*, pp. 27-31) to see that his visit to London had not increased his zeal for the service in which he was to take part. That service had now assumed a definite form. Essex, whose late disaster in Cornwall had been handsomely condoned in the general respect for him, was again to be in command of an army, and Waller and Manchester were to co-operate with him in such a way as to meet and oppose the King returning eastwards to Oxford, and frustrate at the same time any movement of Rupert's. In reality, Essex, sick at heart, was to leave the conduct of this war to his co-generals, Waller and Manchester. To march west, therefore, was still the injunction to Manchester from the Derby House Committee. "Your Lordship was present at our debates and do know the necessity of this service," they write to him September 24. Manchester's reply from Harefield on the 25th is characteristic. The bridge at Maidenhead, by which he meant to pass the Thames, was broken; "this also being the Fast-day, I thought it my duty to seek God;" but—

Your Lordships may be assured that I shall march as soon as with any conveniency I can, and therefore I shall desire that favour from your Lordships that my former observances to your commands may somewhat prevail in lessening the opinions of my backwardness to obey your commands. I was present at some of the debates which your Lordships mention, and your Lordships know what my humble opinion was. I am still of the same mind—that, if the King be upon his march, in that condition that I see those armies in, you expose us to scorn, if not to ruin; but, my Lords, when my sense is delivered, I shall obey as far as in me lies.

On the 29th of September he is at Reading, Cromwell's horse-detachment then to the north of him about Oxford; and from Reading he does not budge for more than a fortnight. Again his correspondence with the Committee (pp. 31-46) is worth study. One sees his heart back in his own Eastern Association, the hardships of the various counties of which by the removal of the army beyond their bounds he represents most carefully; and, though he is still profuse in expressions of obedience, he finds excuse after excuse for not marching farther west. Once (October 2) the Committee are irritated to this reply :—

Having taken into consideration how prejudicial delays have always proved to the public service, and how necessary it is that your Lordship should advance speedily westward, we have thought fit again to renew our desires to your Lordship to send your horse and foot according to our former orders; which we hope you will do with that expedition that we shall not need to iterate it again to your Lordship.

Notwithstanding this and more to the same effect,[a] Manchester, on the 14th of October, was still at Reading. On the 19th, however, in consequence of consultation with Waller, and in order to a conjunction with Essex's army, he was at Basingstoke in Hants, where

[a] Although the Committee of the two Kingdoms at Derby House was really the authorised organ of Parliament in war matters and its missives were in effect orders from Parliament, it is worth noting that the House of Commons itself took notice of Manchester's dilatoriness at this time. Among Mr. Bruce's jottings of material for the continuation of his Preface I find two extracts from the Commons Journals illustrating this fact. On the 8th of October, *à propos* of a petition from the Committee of the county of Norfolk representing the danger to which that county and others of the Eastern Association were liable " from the moving of the Associated Forces so far westward," the House ordered " That the Earl of Manchester do march with his forces forthwith into the West, for the safety of the public, and consequently of each particular county, according to the direction of the Committee of both Kingdoms; and that this House will take care of the safety of the county of Norfolk and the other Associated Counties in like manner as they will of the rest of the kingdom : And it is referred to the Committee of both Kingdoms to take care herein, and to send this order to the Earl of Manchester." It was duly sent the same day (see No. 46 of the Correspondence); and Manchester, in his reply to the Committee next day (No. 47), notices the fact rather tetchily, thus: "I have often received orders from the House of Commons for my marching westward; but they never designed any place to which I should march." This must have been communicated to the House; for, on the 10th of October, there was a report there on the whole subject of the correspondence between the Earl and the Committee, with a significant note that the first letter to him asking him to expedite his march into the West had been as far back as August 27th, and the House then renewed its order that he should advance and join with the Lord General's and Sir William Waller's forces, referring it to the Derby House Committee to appoint the places of rendezvous. The Committee did not fix the place themselves, but instructed Manchester to communicate with the Lord General on the subject (Nos. 48 and 49); and it came at last to be Basingstoke. In contrast with the entries in the Commons Journals at this date relating to Manchester are those relating to Cromwell. They are about a supply of "pistols and holsters," with " heads," " backs," and " breasts," which Cromwell wanted for his own regiment, and about the mode of raising money for the same. It is rather interesting to note that the person charged with seeing them sent down to Cromwell is Colonel Walton.

the siege of Basing House was in progress. The Committee of Derby House had by this time sent two of their number, the Scottish Sir Archibald Johnston of Warriston and the English Mr. John Crewe, to attend the movements of the generals and stimulate them; and these two civilians, we find (No. 56), met Manchester at Basingstoke. In fact, we are now within sight of the SECOND BATTLE OF NEWBURY.

This battle, so called from Newbury in Berks, where there had been a battle about a year before, was fought on Sunday the 27th of October, 1644. The King's army, commanded by himself and Prince Maurice (Rupert not having come up), was not nearly so numerous as the combined armies of the Parliament, commanded, in Essex's absence, by Manchester and Waller, with Skippon, Sir William Balfour, Lieutenant-General Middleton, Lieutenant-General Cromwell, and Major-General Crawford, among the chief officers under them. The battle lasted three hours, and ended, in the moonlight, in what was thought a victory for the Parliament, but of such a kind that the King marched away easily enough to Wallingford, and thence to Oxford, having previously deposited his cannon and baggage in Donnington Castle, a strong place holding out for him close to Newbury. Nothing was done in the way of pursuit; Donnington Castle remained untaken; nay, twelve days afterwards, when his Majesty returned in full force, Rupert now with him, to relieve and revictual Donnington Castle and recover his ordnance and baggage, he was permitted to do so (November 8). The Parliamentary generals declined also another pitched battle to which he subsequently dared them on the old Newbury ground, and let him return to Oxford in leisurely triumph. The war was then over for the year, the armies on both sides preparing to go into winter quarters.[a]

The disappointment in Parliament, and in London generally, was extreme. On the 29th of October the Parliament had ordered days of commemoration and thanksgiving in the churches for the

[a] Rushworth, v. 721-730, and Nos. 59-68 of *Manchester's Correspondence*.

"great and good success" at Newbury, and for another recent success in the capture of Newcastle by the Scottish auxiliary army (October 19); but the subsequent news, and especially that of the King's triumph in the Donnington Castle affair, had changed their mood.

My Lord and Gentlemen,
We have received your letters concerning the relief of Donnington Castle by the enemy, and are very sorry that they met not with that opposition that was expected from an army that God had blessed lately with so happy a victory against them:

these opening words of a letter addressed, November 12, by the Derby House Committee to the Earl of Manchester and his fellow-commanders (No. 69 of *Correspondence*), are the prologue to a great impeachment, in which it is Manchester that is the chief defendant, and it is Cromwell that steps out to take him by the throat. The essence of the story as far as to the 25th of November lies in the following extracts from the Commons Journals, which I find among Mr. Bruce's miscellaneous jottings, carefully written out, partly in his own hand, partly in another:—

Nov. 13. *Ordered*, That the Members of this House that are of the Committee of both Kingdoms do to-morrow give an account to this House concerning the carriage of the business at the relieving of Donnington Castle near Newbury by the King's forces.

Nov. 14. Sir Arthur Hasilrig[a] related unto the House the passages of the whole business concerning the relieving of Donnington Castle by the King's forces.—Mr. Solicitor [St. John] was ready, for the Committee of both Kingdoms, to give an account to the House of relieving Donnington Castle, according to an order yesterday made: But, the House having formerly received a relation made by Sir Arthur Hasilrig of that business, Mr. Solicitor proceeded not to his Report.

[a] He was a member of the Committee of both Kingdoms, had been present at the Battle of Newbury, and had just been sent to town by Manchester, Waller, and Sir William Balfour, as joint commanders, to give the Committee "a right understanding" of the Donnington Castle business. (See No. 68 of *Correspondence*.)

Nov. 19. Resolved, &c., That it be referred to the Committee of both Kingdoms to consider the state and condition of all the armies and forces under the command of the Parliament, and to put them into such a posture as may make them most useful and advantageous to the Kingdom.

Nov. 22. *Ordered*, That the Members of this House that are of the Committee of both Kingdoms do to-morrow give an account to this House of the whole carriage and motions of the armies, both near Donnington Castle, Newbury, Basinghouse, and of the present posture of them.

Nov. 23. *Ordered*, That it be referred to the Committee of both Kingdoms forthwith to put the armies into such a posture as may keep the line as large as may be, and may oppose the advance of the King's forces, and prevent the enlarging of his quarters: And likewise, upon the consideration of the present state and condition of the armies, as now disposed and commanded, to consider of a Frame or Model of the whole Militia, and present it to the House, as may put the forces into such posture as may be most advantageous for the service of the public. This to be done notwithstanding any former Ordinance of Parliament.

Same Day. Ordered, and the House doth enjoin, That Sir William Waller and Lieutenant-General Cromwell do on Monday morning next declare unto the House their whole knowledge and informations of the particular proceedings of the armies since their conjunction.

On Monday, the 25th of November, accordingly, both Waller and Cromwell did, in their places in the House, make the required statements. What was the nature of Waller's statement is hardly known; all the interest was centred in Cromwell's. It was a bold outbreak, at last, of all that he had been thinking about Manchester for months, and nothing less than a sustained and deliberate impeachment of that Earl. The sole accessible record of it hitherto, however, in the form of a report of Cromwell's speech, has been the summary given in Rushworth, as follows:—

That the said Earl hath always been indisposed and backward to engagements, and against ending of the war with the sword, and for such a peace to which a victory would be a disadvantage; and hath declared this by principles express to that purpose, and a continued series of carriage and actions answerable. That, since the taking of York, as if the Parliament had now advantage full enough, he hath declined whatever tended to further advantage upon the enemy; neglected and studiously shifted off opportunities to that purpose, as if he thought the King too low and the Parliament too high,—especially at Donnington Castle. That he hath drawn the army into, and detained them in, such a posture as to give the enemy great advantages; and this *before* his conjunction with the other armies [*i.e.*, with Essex's and Waller's just before Newbury], by his own absolute will, against or without his Council of War, against many commands from the Committee of both Kingdoms, and with contempt and vilifying of those commands; and *since* the conjunction, sometimes against the Councils of War, and sometimes persuading and deluding the Council to neglect one opportunity with pretence of another, and that again of a third, and at last by persuading that it was not fit to fight at all.[a]

Through Mr. Bruce's diligence, the entire charge of which this is an abstract has now been recovered and is printed for the first time in this volume (pp. 78–95). It is entitled "*An Accompt of the effect and substance of my Narrative made to this House for soe much thereof as concerned the Earl of Manchester*," and is doubtless the reduction to writing immediately by Cromwell himself, in consultation with his friends, of those parts of his speech which the House required to have in that shape for further proceedings.[b] The reader will turn to it with no ordinary interest, and will find it to be a continuous and scathing criticism, paragraph after paragraph,

[a] Rushworth, v. 732.

[b] I cannot agree with the opinion expressed in the last footnote to *Cromwell's Narrative* (p. 95), that the "terseness and perspicuity" of the document are qualities that must have been imparted to it by those who assisted him in drawing it up. In any document in the preparation of which Cromwell took part I should say that the tersest and most emphatic parts, and essentially the most perspicuous, were always *his*. Substantially and throughout, this Narrative appears to me to be Cromwell's own, with suggestions from Haselrig, and perhaps from Waller.

of Manchester's military conduct, from his parting with the armies of Fairfax and the Scots in Yorkshire after Marston Moor (July 1644) to his conjunction with the armies of Essex and Waller in the South for the second battle of Newbury, and the abortive issue of that conjunction in the affair of Donnington Castle (Nov. 1644). We have already given the purport of the document as far as to the beginning of that slow and reluctant movement of the Earl out of his comfortable dormancy in the Eastern Counties which did bring him at last into conjunction with Essex and Waller. Cromwell, however, devotes more space to Manchester's delinquencies in the sequel. Why had the Earl, after his long and obdurate stay at Reading in October, marched southwards to Basingstoke, as if that were the place for a proper conjunction, instead of directly westwards, where Sir William Waller was anxiously expecting him, and whither the orders of the Houses and of the Derby House Committee had so pressingly pointed him? Had he thus marched westward, the conjunction of the three armies might easily have been at Salisbury; in which case the issue of the campaign would have been different—the King still to the west of Salisbury river, without a foot of ground on the other side of it, except two or three Royalist towns and castles, hard beset by the Parliament! Then the neglects and delays between the conjunction at Basingstoke and the Battle of Newbury, including one actual proposal of retreat, from the disgrace of which, Manchester now acting as Commander-in-Chief, the armies were saved only by the remonstrances of Waller and Sir Arthur Hasilrig! Then at the Battle of Newbury itself what blunders of the Earl, what avoiding of the part he had expressly undertaken in the battle, so that the battle was rendered less effective than it might have been; and, above all, when the battle had been won, what dogged opposition to the earnest requests of Waller, Hasilrig, and Cromwell himself, that the whole army should be marched Oxford-ways in pursuit of the King, or at least that Manchester would lend some foot to assist the horse in pursuit! " Neither would be granted, his Lordship expressing extreme unwillingness thereto, making excuses and delays, speaking for his return into his Association, and much for peace." For the next twelve days it had been the same, the Earl either refusing to move, or always making little movements the wrong way, thus positively playing into the hands of the King, and making his return and his relief of Donnington Castle not only possible but easy! And at the last moment, when, after the relief of Donnington Castle, there was the chance of relieving all by another great battle with the King, how had the Earl acted?

His Lordship, having now no further evasion left to shift it off under another name, plainly declared himself against fighting, and, having spent much time in viewing the enemy while they drew off, and preparatory discourses, a council being called, he made it the question whether 'twere prudent to fight. With all earnestness and solicitousness he urged all discouragements against it, opposed all that was said for it. And, amongst other things, it being urged that, if we now let the King go off with such honour, it would give him reputation both at home and abroad . . . but if we beat him now it would lose him everywhere . . . his Lordship, replying, told the council he would assure them there was no such thing, adding (with vehemence) this principle against fighting: that, if we beat the King ninety-nine times, he would be King still, and his posterity, and we subjects still; but, if *he* beat *us* but once, we should be hanged and our posterity be undone. Thus it was concluded not to fight.

On the whole Cromwell could come to no other conclusion than that which he had expressed at the outset of his narrative: viz., that the Earl of Manchester was the man in England most blameable for recent mishaps, and that his " backwardness to all action " had proceeded not so much from dullness of mind as from a rooted " principle of unwillingness " to see the Parliament too successful. Whitlocke's recollection of Cromwell's narrative is that it " gave great satisfaction to the Commons," and that, in the matter of Donnington Castle, it " seemed, but cautiously enough, to lay more blame on the Lord-General's army [Essex's] than upon any other."

The second statement may refer to portions of Cromwell's speech in the House apart from that charge against Manchester which alone it was necessary to reduce to writing; and the first statement seems quite authentic. The Commons Journals for Nov. 25, 1644, show what occurred immediately after Waller and Cromwell had addressed the House. The whole business was referred for inquiry and report to a Committee of the House, previously appointed for army matters, of which Mr. Zouch Tate, one of the members for Northampton, was chairman; and this Committee was empowered to examine witnesses and send for all necessary papers, including letters despatched or received by the Committee of both Kingdoms.

The Earl of Manchester must have known pretty exactly that same day all that had happened in the Commons. *His* place for replying was, of course, in the House of Lords—not now, it is to be remembered, that unbroken body of 150 peers, temporal and spiritual, which had existed before the Civil War, but the mere Parliamentarian fragment of it, consisting of about thirty peers in all, of whom seldom more than fifteen were present. Here, for the first time since his return from his campaign, Manchester appeared on the 26th of November, the day after Cromwell's impeachment of him in the other House; and the Lords Journals of that and the few following days show the steps taken by him and his brother peers:—

Tuesday, Nov. 26.—The Earl of Manchester signified to this House " That, since he attended this House last, he hath had the honour to be in employment in some of the armies of Parliament, and some actions of the army where his lordship was hath not given satisfaction to some; an account whereof he will be ready to give to this House when he shall be appointed." And this House appointed Thursday next for his Lordship to give this House an account thereof.

Thursday, Nov. 28.—The Earl of Manchester made to this House a large narrative of the carriage of the affairs of the army at Newbury, and of some speeches spoken by Lieutenant-Colonel [*sic*] Cromwell, which concerns much the honour of this House and the Peers of England, and the good and interest between the two kingdoms of England and Scotland.

Hereupon the House nominated these Lords Committees following, to consider what is fit to be done upon that which the Earl of Manchester delivered this day to this House :—Lord General [the Earl of Essex], Lord Admiral [the Earl of Warwick], the Earl of Northumberland, the Earl of Pembroke, the Earl of Salisbury, Lord North. Any three to meet this afternoon, at three of the clock, in the Lord Keeper's lodgings.

Monday, Dec. 2.—The Earl of Manchester acquainted the House, " That he having made a Narrative to their Lordships concerning the business of the affairs of the army at Newbury and other affairs, and by their Lordships commanded to put it down in writing, which he has accordingly done, and is ready to present it to the House:" Which the House received, and caused it to be read (*Here enter them.*)—the narrative being of two parts, one concerning the business touching the affairs of the army at Donnington Castle, the other concerning Lieutenant-General Cromwell.

The House being satisfied with the Earl of Manchester's Narrative concerning the affairs of the army at Donnington Castle, there being nothing appearing to the contrary, it is Ordered, To communicate the same to the House of Commons. And that narrative concerning Lieutenant-Colonel [*sic*] Cromwell, in regard he is a member of the House of Commons, the House resolved, To communicate the narrative to them at a Conference; and the Lord Wharton and the Lord North are appointed to read the papers at the Conference.

A message was sent to the House of Commons by Mr. Serjeant Whitfield and Mr. Sergeant Fynch, to desire a Conference, so soon as it may stand with their conveniency, in the Painted Chamber, [1.] Touching a Narrative concerning the affairs of the army at Donnington Castle ; 2. Concerning a Narrative wherein a member of their House is concerned.

Ordered [while the two sergeants are away to the Commons requesting a Conference of the two Houses], That these Lords following are appointed to join with a proportionable number of the House of Commons to examine the business of the army at Donnington Castle and the proceedings thereof:—Lord General, Lord Admiral, Earl of Northumberland, Earl of Pembroke, Earl of Salisbury, Earl of Denbigh, Lord North: any three. The Speaker [of the Lords] was to let them [the Commons] know at the Conference " that their Lordships have appointed seven lords

HISTORICAL PREFACE.   lxxiii

to examine the business of the army at Donnington Castle, and the proceedings thereof, and to desire that the House of Commons would appoint a proportionable number of their House to join with them in the said examination. For the latter part, in regard it concerned a member of their House, their Lordships have forborne to proceed in the business, as being of a high nature, until their Lordships had communicated the business to them [the Commons].[a]

Both the Lords Journals and those of the Commons show that the conference of the two Houses so requested was held that same day (Dec. 2), and that consequently the Commons were then put in possession of the two distinct documents which Manchester had presented to the Lords as embodying what he had already delivered to them orally: viz. (1) His counter-narrative of recent military events, in exculpation of himself from the charges of Cromwell and others; and (2) A serious charge against Cromwell personally on account of speeches said to have been uttered by him, at various times, derogatory to the House of Lords and the whole order of the Peerage, and tending also to offend the Scots and disturb the good understanding between the two nations.

The first of these Papers has been preserved, and is given in Rushworth, where it fills four folio pages (v. 733-736). Godwin finds reason for thinking that it was penned by Denzil Holles; but it is, at all events, in a studiously calm and dignified style, quite befitting the character of the Earl himself. He begins with the Battle of Newbury and the subsequent affair of Donnington Castle, as the transactions in which he had been most distinctly blamed. His defence, in general, is in these words:—

From the time I came to join with my Lord General's army I never did anything without joint consent of those that were the best experienced

[a] These extracts from the Lords Journals I take from Mr. Bruce's MS. collection of materials for his preface; and I have not thought it necessary, with his careful copies before me, to refer to the originals. I adhere to the copies even where they keep the faulty grammar of the original, only translating the usual *Comes* of the Journals into "Earl," or the like.

CAMD. SOC.   *l*

and chiefest commanders in all the armies; and herein I shall appeal to those who were sent down from the Committee of both Kingdoms whether upon all debates my expressions were not these, "I cannot pretend to have any experience in this way; therefore what *you* shall resolve *I* shall observe;" and I am confident that both they and all the commanders of the Army will justify my practice made good my professions.

In the particulars of his version of the facts, however, there is a continual pointing to Cromwell as one who had thwarted commands and failed in duty. Thus, at Newbury Battle, the Earl himself had done all he had undertaken, and other parts of the army had behaved in such a way as to contribute to the success; "but where those horses were that Lieutenant-General Cromwell commanded I have as yet had no certain account." Then, afterwards, on the news of the King's return from Oxford for the relief of Donnington Castle, when the Earl, after consulting with Skippon, thought a rendezvous of all the dispersed horse necessary, and had sent orders to that effect to Sir William Balfour and Cromwell, what had Cromwell done?

He came unto me, and in a discontented manner expressed himself, asking me whether I intended to *flay* my horse; for, if I called them to a rendezvous [after so much hard work recently], I might have their *skins*, but no *service* from them. I told him my opinion was that it was absolutely necessary, for, if it were not done, I doubted if we should have them present when we had most use of them; yet, he persisting in his dislike of it, I told him he might do as he pleased.

Again, when the King had relieved Donnington Castle and threatened battle, why had the army been obliged to remain on the defensive and confine itself to repelling with its foot the charge of the enemy? Because, though "some of my Lord General's horse and some of Sir William Waller's" were on the side of the river where the action was, "Lieutenant-General Cromwell had not brought over any horse, notwithstanding I had desired him that all of them might be drawn over on that side of the river." The Earl then touches on the capital charge of his allowing the King after all to retreat undisturbed instead of compelling him to a battle. That had been done, he declares, by the unanimous consent of all the commanders assembled in council, on the ground that a defeat of the Parliamentary army at that time, with the Scottish auxiliaries and other forces so far away in the north, might be fatal; and, in taking that view himself, he had only agreed with others, and especially with Sir Arthur Hasilrig. Here he reverts to his general defence of having always acted by advice; after which, in two brief closing paragraphs, he goes back to topics of older date than his conjunction with Essex's army and Waller's. He had been blamed for dilatoriness at Lincoln and neglect of the orders of the Committee of both Kingdoms to hasten southward and westward in order to that conjunction. Lieutenant-General Cromwell himself could be an efficient witness in answer to that charge, if he would recollect certain particulars. Finally, about certain "discontents" which "brake forth" in his army of the Associated Counties and were really "the cause of retarding that service," the Earl does not think it necessary to speak until desired to do so.

The contemporary and more secret paper, containing Manchester's report of highly inflammatory sayings in which Cromwell had for some time been indulging, has not come down in the Journals of either House, or in any of the collections; nor, unfortunately, has Mr. Bruce's research recovered it. We have the means of guessing, however, what was the nature of those utterances of Cromwell here and there in his wrath which were now remembered against him and gathered into one mass by Manchester to be hurled at his head. With others of the Independents and forward spirits he had observed that the shred of a House of Lords nominally adhering to Parliament, and still acting as an Upper House with all the pomp and forms that had belonged to that House in its complete state, was really a clog on the energies of the other House, impeding what was proposed there, and causing languour and half-heartedness in the war. How was it possible for men of large estates and great family interests to avoid making the safety of those estates and interests a prime consideration in all their debates and methods, and so looking forward anxiously to any reconciliation with the King that would restore the *status quo antè*, with only the few changes deemed indispensable? Perceiving this, Cromwell had begun to doubt whether the war would ever be finished until the fragment of the House of Peers had been swept out of the way; and he had, perhaps, pushed his speculation farther, and begun to question the desirableness of any peerege whatever, or at least any peerage of the existing sort, in the future constitution of England. Never afraid of bold speaking, and indeed liable, on occasion, to sudden gusts and phrenzies of expression, he had talked in this strain among his friends, and perhaps sometimes in more miscellaneous company. At least once, it appears, whether in passionate earnestness or in a moment of semi-humorous confidence, he had surprised Manchester himself with some outbreak of the kind.

General Cromwell declared to the Earl of Manchester his hatred of the Nobility and House of Peers, wishing there was never a *lord* in England, and saying he loved such and such because they loved not *lords*, and that it would not be well till he [Edward Montagu, Earl of Manchester] was but *Mr. Montagu*.

Such is the record, long afterwards, in Holles's memoirs,[a] repeating, perhaps, one of the anecdotes of Cromwell that figured in Manchester's present paper. But we have a more exact and complete description of the contents of the paper, written at the very moment by one who was at the centre of information and in all the secrets of the Presbyterian party—the Scottish Commissioner Baillie. "Always, my Lord Manchester," writes Baillie, December 1, to Scotland, " has cleared himself abundantly to the House of Lords, and there has recriminate Cromwell as one who has avowed his desire to abolish the Nobility of England ; who has spoken contumeliously of the Scots' intention of coming to England to establish

[a] P. 18, as quoted in Parl. Hist. iii. 349.

their Church government (in which Cromwell said he would draw his sword against them)—also against the Assembly of Divines; and has threatened to make a party of Sectaries, to extort by force, both from King and Parliament, what conditions they thought meet."[a] The Scots, therefore, with their pertinacious pushing of their Presbyterian system in all its strictness upon England, and their loan of their vaunted auxiliary army solely for that end, had become, equally with the English Nobility, a subject of Cromwell's comments; and, despite his union with them in the *Solemn League and Covenant*, his comments on them, and on the Westminster Assembly as virtually their organ, had been growing more and more disrespectful. In bringing this out in his paper, Manchester had done a most politic thing in his own interest. The little phalanx of Scots then in London, as members of the Committee of both Kingdoms, lay Commissioners for other purposes, or Divines in the Westminster Assembly, were a very powerful body, not to be insulted with impunity. They had long looked askance on Cromwell as the champion of Independency, and now was their time for action. " It's like, for the interest of our nation," proceeds Baillie in the same letter, "we must crave reason of that Darling of the Sectaries, and in obtaining his removal from the army (which himself by his over-rashness has procured) to break the power of that potent faction. This is our present difficile exercise: we had need of your prayers." To understand what was really meant by this, we must turn to Whitlocke.

In the lull in military operations caused by the retirement of the several armies into winter quarters, propositions for peace had again been revived. Commissioners from the two Houses, with some of the Scottish Commissioners, had gone from London (Nov. 20) with overtures to the King at Oxford; they had had interviews with him, and had brought back answers; and matters were thus in train for that great TREATY OF UXBRIDGE which occupies so much space, with such a zero of result, in the history of the Civil War.

[a] Baillie, ii. 245.

It was a crisis, therefore, when the various elements in the leadership of what had all along been the more Conservative party among the Parliamentarians—Essex and his stately brother peers, Holles and his Presbyterian associates in the Commons, and the Scottish Commissioners—might well unite in an attempt to disgrace and disable such a representative of the more revolutionary party as Cromwell. He was in London, away from his Ironsides, and again for the time a mere Member of Parliament; and had not his quarrel with Manchester given them the opportunity? Why not convert Manchester's charge against him in the Lords into a public State prosecution to be regularly tried at law? This, in fact, was the " difficile exercise" in which, Baillie tells us, he and his fellow-Scots in London were engaged, and for success in which he begged the prayers of his co-Presbyters in Scotland. Probably because it failed, we hear little more of it from Baillie; but a passage in Whitlocke supplies the deficiency. It is that famous passage where Whitlocke describes a private conference held at Essex House in the Strand within a few days after the date of Baillie's letter. Summoned to Essex House, "one evening very late," by an urgent message from the lord of the mansion, but not knowing on what business, Whitlocke and his fellow-lawyer Maynard, we are told, found a small company already with the Lord General, consisting of " the Scots Commissioners, Mr. Holles, Sir Philip Stapleton, Sir John Meyrick [three of the leading Presbyterians of the Commons], and divers other friends." After some preliminaries, the Scottish Chancellor Loudoun, at the request of Essex, opened to the two lawyers the purpose of the meeting. He did so very warily, and in his peculiar Scottish dialect, which Whitlocke tries to reproduce. " Ye ken vary weele that Lieutenant-General Cromwell is no friend of ours;" " he not only is no friend to us and to the government of our Church, but he is also no well-wisher to his Excellency [Essex], whom you and we all have cause to love and honour:"—these are two of his reported expressions, with the addition: " It is thought requisite for us, and for the carrying on of the cause of the tway kingdoms, that this obstacle or remora may be removed out of the way." Could this be done? In Scotland there would have been no difficulty in such a case. By the law of Scotland any *incendiary* might be brought to trial; and " we clepe him an *incendiary* whay kindleth coals of contention and raises differences in the State to the public damage." Now in the *Solemn League and Covenant* between the two nations this word had been adopted—one of the paragraphs of that document expressly binding both nations " to endeavour the discovery of such as have been or shall be incendiaries," that they might be brought to public trial. But did the law of England recognise the kind of criminal called an incendiary, and provide means for bringing him to account? This was the point on which the Scots desired the judgment of Whitlocke and Maynard. " Whether your law be the same or not you ken best, who are mickle learned therein." Both Whitlocke and Maynard assured the company in reply that the law of England did recognise *incendiaries* and could deal with them; but they both suggested serious doubts as to the proposal to bring Cromwell within that category. They were not aware of proofs against him sufficient for the purpose; the collection of such proofs would be difficult; he was a man of great parts, and great interest in the Commons and throughout the country; it would not do for persons in such high authority as the Lord General and the Scottish Commissioners to appear in such a business unless they could be sure of success. Here, Whitlocke adds, Holles, Stapleton, and some others, struck smartly in, mentioning acts and words of Cromwell's that ought to prove him an incendiary, denying his great interest in the Commons, and urging immediate procedure. The Scottish Commissioners, however, had been convinced by the reasoning of the English lawyers, and thought it would be better to wait and collect more proofs. With this conclusion the meeting broke up " about two o'clock in the morning;" and Whitlocke " had some cause to believe that at this debate some who were present were false brethren, and informed Cromwell of all that had passed." At all events, Cromwell, though he never mentioned the subject, seemed to know that Whitlocke and Maynard had done him a service.[a]

The idea of a State prosecution of Cromwell having been abandoned, his quarrel with Manchester, in its two forms of his charge against Manchester and Manchester's recrimination upon him, was left to the ordinary course of process through the two Houses. Or rather, through the whole of December, it was left to the course arranged for it by the Commons, the Lords waiting the result of their conference with that House of December 2nd. It becomes evident also that the two Houses tended more and more to opposite moods in the business, the Commons on the whole (notwithstanding the number of Presbyterians in the House) leaning somehow to Cromwell, while the Lords were disposed to protect and abet Manchester.

The state of the business in the Commons immediately after the proceedings at the conference with the other House had been formally reported (which was done by Mr. Holles, December 4) had been this :—The Committee, of which Mr. Zouch Tate was chairman, already entrusted with the duty of investigating Cromwell's charges against Manchester, was to proceed in that duty, sending for papers, examining witnesses, &c., all under strict injunction of secrecy, and never fewer than eight of the Committee to be present. But for that new form of the business which had been occasioned by Manchester's exculpation of himself and counter-charge against Cromwell in the Lords, and by the communication of both to the Commons at the conference, another Committee had been appointed, with the significant instruction that they were " to consider whether the Privilege of this House be broken by the matter of this Report made by Mr. Holles, and to present to the House some expedient for putting the same into a way of examination." Eighteen members had been named for this Committee, December 4, among whom were Holles and other violent Presbyterians, but also Whitlocke and Maynard, with St. John, Vane, Hasilrig, and others, naturally

[a] Whitlocke, ed. 1853, i. 343-348.

favourable to Cromwell; and the number had been increased, December 7, by the addition of eighteen more, of different shades of opinion (Stapleton one of them), and "all the lawyers of the House." Of this second and larger Committee, already in existence probably when four at least of its members took part in the private meeting at Essex House, the chairman was Mr. John Lisle, member for Winchester.

Through the rest of December we are to conceive the two Committees more or less busy, each over its appointed work. Of the proceedings of MR. LISLE'S COMMITTEE, which involved the question of privilege between the two Houses, we hear nothing through the month; but of those of MR. TATE'S COMMITTEE, entrusted with the investigation of Cromwell's charges against Manchester, we do learn something in the document recovered by Mr. Bruce, and printed in the present volume under the title of *Notes of Evidence against the Earl of Manchester*. They are brief and unconnected memoranda of the evidence given in support of Cromwell's charges by a number of witnesses that had been called before the Committee. Cromwell and Waller themselves, it appears, had been among those witnesses; but Hasilrig, and such officers in Manchester's army as Hammond, Ireton, Harrison, Rich, Jones, Wilson, Hooper, Norton, Pickering, and Desborough, had also been examined. The particulars to which they testified, and how they fit into the story of Manchester's alleged "backwardness to all action," will be gathered best from a perusal of the Notes. So far as the Notes bear, the evidence had as yet been all on Cromwell's side, or in support of the prosecution, and there had been no evidence for the defence.

It is not to be supposed, however, that the Earl of Manchester and his friends were inactive. That the Earl was collecting materials both for his own defence and for the verification of his counter-charge against Cromwell appears from the fact that there have survived among his papers at Kimbolton the two documents, procured by Mr. Bruce, which are printed in this volume under the titles *Narrative of the Earl of Manchester's Campaign* and *Statement by an Opponent of Cromwell*. It is possible indeed that he may have had one or both of these in his possession before he made his charge against Cromwell in the Lords on the 28th of November, and that they may have supplied him with some of the particulars included in that charge; but it is as likely that they came to him after that charge was made and Mr. Tate's Committee and Mr. Lisle's were exploring the matter for the other House. In either case, they fall to be noticed here:—

1. *Narrative of the Earl of Manchester's Campaign.* This, as we already know, was nothing else than a statement by Manchester's Scottish Major-General Crawford, hastening to the rescue of his chief, and glad of the opportunity of saying his worst at some length against his old opponent Cromwell. The substance of it, as far as to Manchester's march from Lincoln, with a view to the conjunction of his army with those of Essex and Waller in the west, has already been given; and it is only necessary now to note the substance of the rest. It is exactly in the strain of the preceding, the same virulent antipathy to Cromwell breaking out, sentence after sentence, through the same feeble and confused style of narration and the same inexpertness in grammar. Manchester to blame for the incompleteness of the success at Newbury, or for the neglect of the pursuit of the King's forces after the battle! Why, Manchester had behaved beautifully, and it was Cromwell that was in both cases the real culprit. It was the *horse* of the army that never were where they ought to have been, and never were willing to do what they might have done; and to whom was that to be ascribed but to Cromwell and his under-officers? Then as to the return of the King, his relief of Donnington Castle, his safe retreat without battle again offered to him, and that lame conclusion of the campaign about which Cromwell and others were now crying out! All through this tissue of affairs too the backward man had still been Cromwell, with his precious horse, either out of the way when they were wanted or reported by him as too weak for action. Major-General

Crawford himself had at one critical moment pointed out to Cromwell a way in which his horse might have done real service, and he had declined the hint. And, at the Council of War, where it had been decided to allow the King to retreat without battle, who had been the chief advocates of that policy? Why, Sir Arthur Hasilrig and Cromwell, the first arguing that the King was too strong and that a battle with him might be disastrous, and Cromwell following with "a speech very near a quarter of an hour" to the same effect. Finally, as to Cromwell's accusation against Manchester that he had acted without advice of Councils of War or against such advice, Crawford would recall one memorable incident. When letters had come to the Army showing the extreme dissatisfaction in London with the affair of Donnington Castle and the poor ending of the campaign, and among these letters an official one to Manchester and the other commanders from the Committee of both Kingdoms (No. 69 of the *Correspondence*), Manchester had been vexed by nothing so much as by the insinuation, indirectly conveyed in that letter, that he had not acted duly by advice of Councils of War. What had then happened?"

In my Lord of Manchester's lodging in Newbury, in the presence of my Lord of Manchester, Sir William Balfour, Sir William Waller, Major-General Skippon, Colonel Barklet, and Major-General Crawford, Cromwell did say (finding my Lord of Manchester much moved at the aforesaid letter, after he reads it twice over) that he found nothing in the letter but what may be written without reflection upon any, and told my Lord of Manchester : "My Lord, I hold him for a villain and a knave that would do any man ill offices ; but there was nothing done but what was justifiable and by the consent of the Council of War," and that there was nothing done but what was answerable. So upon that Council of War there was presently thought fit that there should be a letter drawn and sent to the Committee of both Kingdoms representing the whole condition of the army ; which was referred to be done by Lieut.-General Cromwell ; which accordingly *was* done, wherein he gave a full relation of the weakness of the Army; which, considering the ways he has gone, much deserves your notice-taking of it.[a]

2. *Statement by an Opponent of Cromwell.* This is an anonymous document, but reveals itself at once as having been written, for the Earl of Manchester's use, by some Presbyterian colonel or captain of his army who had grudges of old standing against Cromwell. Its peculiarity is that it goes back upon the earlier part of Cromwell's military career, and furnishes black reminiscences of him from the first in his own Eastern Counties. In an evil hour in December 1642, the writer, having property in the Isle of Ely, which he wanted to make safe from war-risks, had gone to his neighbour Cromwell, then only a captain of horse in the district, to ask his advice. The result had been that he had been lured by Cromwell to set up as a captain of dragoons, raising a troop and equipping them at his own charge, and actually paying the troop and his under-officers for ten weeks: "which to this day I have never received one penny." Thus a captain of dragoons almost in spite of himself, and with money invested in the concern, he had continued in the army of the Eastern Association ever since, or at least till near its late junction with the other armies in the west. He had thus, of course, had ample opportunities of observing Crom-

[a] In Manchester's exculpation of himself to the Lords, he also makes a strong point of Cromwell's voluntary burst in his defence on the occasion here mentioned by Crawford: "And I must acknowledge that Lieutenant-General Cromwell was sensible of a contradiction in this particular; as, when there was but an information of such a report cast out of London that I had acted without the advice of the Council of War, he professed that he was a villain and a liar that should affirm any such thing." It is clear that something of the kind must have happened, however it is to be reconciled with what followed. Crawford's farther statement, that Cromwell himself was the draftsman of a letter in the name of the commanders jointly to the Committee of both Kingdoms explaining the whole state of matters, does not appear in the Earl's own narrative. If such a letter still exists, it might be important. Mr. Bruce's collection of copies from the correspondence of the Committee of both Kingdoms contains no such thing. It stops at No. 69, the letter which so much vexed Manchester.

well and knowing his principles. He will, therefore, string together a few facts. Cromwell, when a colonel, had "made choice of his officers, not such as were soldiers or men of estate, but such as were common men, poor and of mean parentage; only he would give them the title of godly precious men." He had heard Cromwell often say that " it must not be soldiers nor Scots that must do this work, but it must be the godly to this purpose." Accordingly he had packed his own regiment, and then others, with Independents. " If you look at his own regiment of horse, see what a swarm there is of those that call themselves the godly: some of them profess they have seen visions and had revelations." Little better with the regiments of Colonels Fleetwood, Russell, Montague, Pickering, and Rainsborough, "all of them professed Independents entire." Once, when he, the writer, had done a good stroke of service at Wisbeach, Cromwell had assumed the credit of it; which was his general habit. He had once told the writer to " hold his tongue," for he " spoke he knew not what." Cromwell had once told him he would " make the Isle of Ely the strongest place in the world, and he would out with all the wretches and ungodly men, and he would place in it godly and precious people, and he would make it a place for God to dwell in " : " yet at this day the Isle is in no [better] posture than it was in at the time he came into it; only it is become a mere Amsterdam," *i. e.* a refuge of all sects, where soldiers occupied the pulpits and the regular ministers dared not preach. " They frequently rebaptize the people of that Isle." Plenty of money had passed through Cromwell's hands; there was at Ely, on the file of letters to the Committee there, one from Cromwell instructing them " to pay to his wife 5*l.* per week towards her extraordinaries " (which had been done for a great while, and " I am sure there is no ordinance of Parliament for *that* "); and yet the writer had never been repaid *his* advances, but had been put off with fair words. He had heard Cromwell talk against "lords." Once, when he was in London, two of Cromwell's troopers and another man had come to him with a petition to Parliament for liberty of conscience, already "with a great many of hands and marks to it," desiring him to sign it.

I was troubled at it and told them I would have my hand cut off before I would set my hand to it, and told them if any nation in the world were in the ready way to Heaven it was the Scots. They told me they thought I had been a godly man, but now they perceive what I was, and went away: ever after Colonel Cromwell did slight me.

The writer had been with Manchester's army at Huntingdon when the news of Essex's flight from Cornwall and the loss of his army there arrived; and he can vouch that the Independents of the army, instead of being cast down, were positively joyful. He hates the Independents, and " can say by experience, The Lord of Heaven deliver every honest man out of their hands!"[a]

Meanwhile the Lords were becoming impatient over the burial of the question between Manchester and Cromwell in the silent procedure of two mere committees of the Commons. Under the date Monday the 30th December, their Journals contain this entry:—

A message was sent to the House of Commons by Mr. Serjeant Whitfield and Mr. Serjeant Fynch, to desire an answer, as soon as it may stand with their conveniency, touching the conference concerning the Narrative touching the Earl of Manchester's business. Mr. Serjeant Whitfield and Mr. Serjeant Fynch return with this answer from the House of Commons: "That they will send an answer concerning the Narrative touching the Earl of Manchester's business by messengers of their own."

---

[a] The writer of this queer statement might perhaps, by some search, be yet identified. Can he have been the "Captain Arminger" mentioned in Crawford's Narrative as one of the officers in Manchester's army opposed to Cromwell and Independency (p. 60), and who was "outed" by Cromwell just after the march from Lincoln had begun (p. 61)? If so, can this "Captain Arminger," by some error of transcript, be the same as the "Captain Margery" of whom we hear in two of Cromwell's letters of September 1643 (Carlyle's *Cromwell*, ed. 1857, i. pp. 134-5 and 139-141), when he and Cromwell were still on friendly terms?

The Commons Journals of the same day exhibit the counterpart entry, but in words implying that the message of the Lords had been rather urgent.[a] The phrase " will send an answer by messengers of their own " in such intercourse between the two Houses meant that the House using it was not prepared with an immediate answer, or with the answer expected; and this was certainly now the case. In fact, by this time, the Quarrel between Manchester and Cromwell had become a far less important thing in the eyes of the Commons, and of Cromwell himself, than it had been three weeks before. It had been engulphed in a much larger business, engrossing the Commons through those three weeks. This was the famous business of THE SELF-DENYING ORDINANCE.

No one that knows anything of Cromwell needs to be told that personal enmity was not the motive to his attack on Manchester That amiable and popular nobleman had simply become, in Cromwell's judgment, a type of the lazy and half-hearted aristocratic generalship that had been the impediment of the Parliamentary cause hitherto, and that must be removed if the cause were to prosper in future. To denounce this style of generalship in one typical example, to blast it out of the army by the publicity and terror of one well-directed personal impeachment, was a legitimate method, were there no other. Seeing no other, Cromwell had ventured on it, with all the risks; he had, at his own peril, been the man to bell the cat. But, after all, might there not be another method, and a less disagreeable one? After he had made his charge against Manchester, and Manchester had made his countercharge, and the two Houses were in perturbation over the affair, this is the question which Cromwell had begun to ask himself. The state of mind of the House of Commons, as shown in recent votes, furnished the necessary hint. Had not the House, in its disgust at the lame ending of the late campaign, referred it to the Committee

[a] As before, Mr. Bruce's MS. copies are my authorities for these entries in the Journals of the Houses.

of both Kingdoms to revise the whole " posture " of the Armies or Militia of Parliament, and consider of a new " frame or model " for the same? Did not this prove that the House was in the humour for a bold measure? What if one were to drop the prosecution of Manchester in particular, and propose that *all* officers of the army belonging to either House of Parliament should, not for reasons personal to any of them, but on grounds of general expediency, retire from their commands? This would get rid of Manchester; it would also get rid of Essex, Sir William Waller, and many more; it would solve the immediate problem of the English Army; and yet it would do so in a way not irritating to the Scots.

Very few days seem to have been spent by Cromwell and his friends in deliberation on the proposal before it was introduced into the House. This had been done on the 9th of December, when Cromwell's charge against Manchester was but a fortnight old. On that day, the House sitting in grand Committee, and very silent for some time, as if expecting something unusual, Cromwell himself had broken the silence. " It is now a time to speak," he had begun, " or for ever hold the tongue. The important occasion now is no less than to save a nation out of a bleeding, nay, almost dying, condition." Then, after some intermediate sentences :—

What do many say, that were friends at the beginning of the Parliament? Even this, that the members of both Houses have got great places and commands, and, what by interest in Parliament, what by power in the army, will perpetually continue themselves in grandeur, and not permit the war speedily to end, lest their own power should determine with it. This that I speak here to our own faces is but what others do utter behind our backs. I am far from reflecting on any. I know the worth of those commanders, members of both Houses, who are yet in power; but, if I may speak my conscience without reflecting upon any, I do conceive, if the Army be not put into another method, and the war more vigorously prosecuted, the people can bear the war no longer, and will enforce you to a dishonourable peace. But this I would recommend to your prudence, Not to insist upon any complaint or oversight of any commander-in-chief upon any occasion whatsoever; for, as I must acknowledge myself guilty of oversights, so I know they can rarely be avoided in military affairs. Therefore, waiving a strict inquiry into the causes of these things, let us apply ourselves to the remedy; which is most necessary. And I hope we have such true English hearts, and zealous affections towards the general weal of our mother country, as no members of either House will scruple to *deny themselves*, and their our private interests, for the public good, nor account it to be a dishonour done to them, whatever the Parliament shall resolve upon in this weighty matter."

The way having thus been prepared by Cromwell, and the actual motion having been made by Mr. Zouch Tate, and seconded by Harry Vane, it was resolved the same day:—

That, during the time of this war, no member of either House shall have or execute any office or command, military or civil, granted or conferred by both or either of the Houses of Parliament, or any authority derived from both or either of the Houses, and that an Ordinance be brought in accordingly.

The SELF-DENYING ORDINANCE, so proposed, was duly brought in. Though opposed by Whitlocke and others, it went through the House with singular rapidity, and was passed December 19. All London was astounded. "The House of Commons, in one hour," writes Baillie, "has ended all the quarrels which was betwixt Manchester and Cromwell, all the obloquies against the General, the grumblings against the proceedings of many members of their House. They have taken all office from all the members of both Houses. This, done on a sudden, in one session, with great unanimity, is still more and more admired by some, as a most wise, necessar, and heroic action; by others as the most rash, hazardous, and unjust action as ever Parliament did. Much may be said on both hands."[b] Baillie's words are suggestive. They show, for one thing, that the Self-denying Ordinance, though a Cromwellian measure, must somehow have had the approval of a large number of the Presbyterians of the House, and that even the Scots in London were perplexed

[a] Carlyle's *Cromwell*, ed. 1857, i. 160-162.   [b] Baillie, ii. 247

about it rather than hostile. They recognise, still more distinctly, that the Ordinance had been offered by Cromwell and his friends, and accepted by the rest, as a means of honourably ending and hushing up the Manchester impeachment and all other personal quarrels. Cromwell's own words in the House, in preparing the way for the Ordinance, illustrate this very remarkably. In almost express terms he asks the House to let him waive his prosecution of Manchester, retire from the disgusting task of recollecting the past oversights or delinquencies of any particular person, and join with them in a larger and better way of attaining the main object. In passing the Ordinance the House doubtless understood that this was the implication; and, when they sent it up to the Lords, it was virtually an appeal to that body whether they would concur in this method of quashing the Manchester prosecution, with much of the same sort, or compel the House to continue that prosecution.

In reminding the Commons on December 30 of the Manchester prosecution, the Lords, who had then the Self-denying Ordinance before them, had in effect intimated that they would rather see the prosecution go on than pass the Ordinance. For the Peers, indeed, the Ordinance was a more terrible test of self-denial than for the Commons: it was like asking them to superannuate themselves and abjure the hereditary and historic rights of their order. Nevertheless, the Commons waited to see definitely how they would act, and put off from day to day the reports from Mr. Tate's Committee and Mr. Lisle's, notwithstanding another request from the Lords for haste in that matter. On Wednesday, January 15, 1644-5, there was no longer such reason for delay; for on that day the Lords rejected the Self-denying Ordinance. On that day, accordingly, the Commons ordered the Reports to be brought in on Friday. On Friday they were put off till Saturday, and on Saturday again till Monday; on which day (January 20, 1644-5) they *were* brought in, as follows:—

Mr. Lisle reports, from the Committee to which it was referred, the opinions of the Committee concerning the Report [December 4] of a conference had with the Lords made by Mr. Holles, touching a narrative made by the Earl of Manchester concerning the business of Donnington Castle, the which reflects in some particulars, by way of charge, in the opinion of the Committee, upon a member of this House—to consider of and examine which narrative . . . the Lords made a Committee and desired this House to appoint a Committee of a proportionable number. He likewise presented from the Committee a paper containing the matter of the narrative delivered by the Lords at the conference concerning the business of Donnington.

Resolved, &c., That the appointing of a Committee by the House of Lords for the examination of the matters contained in the first part of the Report made by Mr. Holles (wherein Lieut.-General Cromwell, a member of the House of Commons, is concerned) in such a manner as is therein expressed, is a breach of privilege, notwithstanding their desiring the House of Commons to join in the same.

Resolved, &c., That the first part of Mr. Holles his Report [*i.e.*, that which contained Manchester's narrative, in exculpation of himself, with incidental references to Cromwell's military conduct] is not to be put into a way of examination, in regard of the breach of privilege.

Resolved, &c., That a Committee of the House of Commons be appointed to examine the particulars contained in the papers now delivered in by the Committee [*i.e.*, the paper first given in by Mr. Lisle, recapitulating in some new form, free from the taint of breach of privilege, the matter of the narrative of the Earl of Manchester].

Resolved, &c., That a Committee of the House of Commons be appointed to consider of the second part of Mr. Holles his Report [*i.e.*, that which referred to the paper of charges, not merely military, but of a high political nature, against Cromwell, with which Manchester had backed his exculpation of himself, and which the Lords had merely communicated to the Commons, without themselves taking any steps in the matter].

Resolved, &c., That this Committee, to which the particulars in the two former votes [*i.e.*, in the two last paragraphs] are referred, be the Committee formally appointed, Decembris 4, to consider of the matter of Mr. Holles his Report of the conference [*i.e.*, Mr. Lisle's Committee: see *ante*, pp. lxxx., lxxxi.].

Resolved, &c., That a conference be desired with the Lords concerning these particulars.

Mr. Lisle [here, it seems, acting for Mr. Zouch Tate, the chairman of the other Committee] further reported the state of the matter of the narrative made, upon the order and injunction of this House, by Lieut.-General Cromwell and Sir William Waller, concerning divers passages and proceedings of the armies, wherein the Earl of Manchester is much concerned, and the state of the proofs upon examination of the business and hearing witnesses by the Committee. He likewise produced a letter, written unto him by the Earl of Manchester, of January 16, desiring that he might know what those informations are that he hears are given in against him at the Committee before the Report made, that he might give satisfaction. [The Lords Journals show that Manchester had leave from that House to write such a letter.] The which were all read, and immediately re-delivered to the Reporter.

Resolved, &c., That the consideration of this Report shall be resumed on this day sevennight.

Ordered, That the Committee of Decembris 4 [Mr. Lisle's], to which Mr. Holles his Report . . was formerly referred, be revived, and meet *de die in diem*, to consider of the particulars this day referred to them.^a

Substantially, these resolutions of the Commons were a rebuke to the Lords. They had been offered, in the Self-denying Ordinance, a large and comprehensive way of hushing up the quarrel between Manchester and Cromwell, and much besides; and they had rejected the Ordinance. Well, in that case, the Commons were prepared still for the narrower and meaner method of procedure. First of all, they would inform the Lords that their manner of receiving and dealing with Manchester's exculpatory narrative, involving, as that narrative did, reflections on a member of the House of Commons,

---

^a As before, these extracts from the Journals are supplied me by Mr. Bruce's collection of MS. memoranda. I observe, however, that he has omitted the following entry, which occurs in the Journals immediately before the last paragraph he has quoted:—" *Ordered*, That the Committee where Mr. Tate has the chair do examine who was the author, printer, and divulger of the book which bears the name of Mr. Simeon Ashe, a minister, and is concerning the business of Newbury and Donnington, and likewise to consider of the particular carriages about the printing and divulging of that book, or the publishing any matter contained therein." This book or pamphlet by Ashe, Manchester's chaplain, might be worth looking after.

was a breach of privilege; but, that having been explained, they were willing to go on with the whole inquiry, both as it regarded Manchester and as it regarded Cromwell, and to prosecute it to the utmost. They had, therefore, reappointed Mr. Lisle's Committee, with fresh instructions; and they had ascertained the progress of the evidence in Mr. Tate's Committee and left that Committee to proceed. All this was to be regretted; but the responsibility lay with the Lords. They and the Earl of Manchester must take the consequences.

In fact, however, the prosecution had now run aground. The last references to it in Mr. Bruce's extracts from the Journals of the Houses are on Jan. 21 and Jan. 22. On the first of these days there was read in the Commons a letter from the Earl of Manchester to the Speaker asking for information as to the charges against him; and on the second, in answer to his request to be heard in person before Mr. Tate's Committee, the Committee were empowered to do as they might think fit. Thenceforward the business disappears. For, though the Self-denying Ordinance had been rejected by the Lords, the Commons had found another way of effecting their great purpose of Army Reform. One reason given by the Lords for hesitating about the Ordinance being that they did not know in what precise shape the army was to be reconstituted, the Commons had met that difficulty by requiring the Committee of both Kingdoms to report at once the NEW MODEL OF THE ARMY which they had been instructed to devise. This had been done on the 9th of January; and by the 28th of January the New Model complete had passed the Commons. According to this New Model the existing armies of the Parliament were to be weeded, consolidated, and re-organised into one compact army of 22,000 men (14,400 foot, 6,600 horse, and 1,000 dragoons), the commander-in-chief of which was to be Sir Thomas Fairfax, and the major-general of which, or third in command, was to be Philip Skippon. The place of Lieutenant-General, or second in command, was left vacant as yet; and, though the Commons had at first designated most of the colonels, it was thought better to refer their appointment to Fairfax with the future sanction of the two Houses. That so sweeping a measure should have emanated from such a body as the Committee of both Kingdoms, containing not only English Presbyterian Peers and Commoners, but also those Scottish Commissioners whose sole or main rule of action was the Presbyterian interest, is certainly remarkable. The Scottish Commissioners, as we have seen, had been exerting themselves for the destruction of Cromwell; and yet they now concurred in a measure framed according to Cromwell's heart.[a] Altogether the juncture was such that the Lords had to yield to the Commons. They demanded, indeed, that there should be no officers or soldiers in the New Model Army that had not signed the *Solemn League and Covenant;* but, a compromise on that subject having been effected, they succumbed Feb. 15, when the NEW MODEL ORDINANCE became law. Possibly it was hoped that the TREATY OF UXBRIDGE, which had been going on since Jan. 30, would render the New Model unnecessary in practice; but any such hope must have ceased Feb. 22, when the treaty

[a] Godwin, in his History of the Commonwealth (i. 403-405), finds an explanation of the changed mood of the Scottish Commissioners in the fact that the Marquis of Argyle, the supreme man of the Scottish Kingdom, and a more subtle and far-seeing politician than any of the rest, had come to London at this crisis. He founds on a passage in Clarendon (p. 541, ed. 1843), where it is said:—" The Marquis of Argyle was now come from Scotland, and sat with the Commissioners of that kingdom. . . . From the time of his coming to the town, the Scottish Commissioners were less vehement in obstructing the Ordinance or the New Modelling of the Army." This, however, is one of Clarendon's hallucinations. Argyle's name was certainly included in the safe conduct given by the King at Oxford, January 21, 1644-5, for those Commissioners from the Parliament and from the Scots that were to treat at Uxbridge; but he never appeared there. He was detained in Scotland by the necessity of opposing the terrible Montrose. His defeat at Inverlochy, the greatest disaster of his military life, was on February 2; and he was in Edinburgh, with the disaster on his mind, for some weeks afterwards. When he did come to London sixteen months later, the opening words of his speech before a Committee of the two English Houses (June 26, 1646) were these:—" Though I have had the honour to be named by the Kingdom of Scotland in all the Commissions which had relation to this Kingdom [of England] since the beginning of the war, yet I had never the happiness to be with your lordships till now."

was broken off, with nothing accomplished. It was then evident that the year 1645 was to be one of continued war, and that the New Model would have abundant work. It was of no use then for the Lords to stand out against the SELF-DENYING ORDINANCE either. That ordinance, in fact, was already realized in the fabric of the New Model; and, accordingly, having been reintroduced into the Commons in a modified form, and having passed there, it received the assent of the Lords April 3, 1645. On the preceding day (April 2) the Earls of Essex and Manchester, with the Earl of Denbigh, had simplified matters by formally resigning their military commands, both Houses agreeing in a vote recognising the high sense of duty shown by "this action of these lords in this conjuncture of time," and resolving " that their services and fortunes " should be taken into consideration, and ways found for expressing "the acceptance and value both Houses have of their faithfulness and industry in the commands and hazards they have undergone for the public good of the kingdom and safety of the Parliament."

Thus, after having been dead for two months and a-half, the Quarrel between Manchester and Cromwell received an honourable burial. The accurate student of English history will note that the termination of this famous quarrel coincides in time with another great event, distinct from that New-Modelling of the Army and that Self-denying Ordinance which gave it directly the *coup de grâce*. This was the ESTABLISHMENT OF THE PRESBYTERIAN SYSTEM IN ENGLAND, the first express votes for which in the two Houses were in January 1644-5. The Independents, having had so much of their own way in army matters, had made this inevitable concession to the general bent of Parliamentarian feeling in Church affairs, satisfied with keeping open the still vital question of the amount of toleration to be granted to Dissenters.

Cromwell, exempted by special vote from the operation of the Self-denying Ordinance, was at once inserted into the New Model Army in that post of Lieutenant-General, or second in command, which had been purposely kept vacant for him. Thence, through successive stages, came the rest of his career, ending in his Protectorship of the United Commonwealth of England, Scotland, and Ireland, with their Colonies and Dominions. Through that great career his quarrel with Manchester was an all but forgotten affair, only heard of now and then when Lilburne and other Levellers reverted to it for their purposes, maintaining that Cromwell ought to have brought Manchester to the scaffold, and that his abandonment of his prosecution of the Earl had been his first step out of the straight path of democratic duty, and the beginning of his truckling with aristocracy and expediency.

Of the Earl himself little more needs here be said. Parliament did remember their promise to take into consideration his past services, and especially his handsome acquiescence at last in the Self-denying Ordinance. In December, 1645, when the successes of the New Model Army had shattered the King's power and brought peace again within view, it was proposed, as part of the terms of the expected peace, that the King should be requested to confer dukedoms on the Earls of Essex, Northumberland, Warwick, and Pembroke, and the honours of the Marquisate on the Earls of Manchester and Salisbury—inferior peerages, with money pensions, to be conferred on others of the Parliamentarian chiefs, including Fairfax, Cromwell, and Waller. As the King, however, would not even then acknowledge himself beaten, that proposal came to nothing; and Manchester, still only as Earl, sat on in his place in the Lords, a leader on the Presbyterian side of the Parliamentarians, and for a while the Speaker of the House, till about the time of the trial and execution of the King. Then, the House of Lords having been abolished to make way for the Commonwealth (February, 1648 9), he retired from the scene, and lived on for about nine years as a mere private and reluctant subject of the Commonwealth, holding no post, except (for a time) that of Chancellor of the University of Cambridge. In 1658, when Cromwell tried the experiment of re-instituting a House of Lords on new principles,

Manchester was one of the few of the old hereditary peers that were summoned to sit in it; but, though he is thus remembered in history as one of "Cromwell's Lords," the honour is merely nominal, as he seems not to have obeyed the summons. When Cromwell's death in that year, and the wreck of the Protectorate of his son Richard, had made the Restoration probable and desirable, Manchester took a very active part in the arrangements for it. Accordingly, after the Restoration, he had a place in the Court and Councils of Charles II. that seemed strangely out of keeping with his antecedents. "That he [Charles II.]," says Clarendon, "might give a lively instance of his grace to those who had been of the party which was faulty, according to his declaration from Breda, he made, of his own free inclination and choice, the Earl of Manchester, who was looked upon as one of the principal heads of the Presbyterian party, Lord Chamberlain of his house; who, continuing still to perform all good offices to his old friends, complied very punctually with all the obligations and duties which his place required, never failed being at chapel, and at all the King's devotions, with all imaginable decency; and, by his extraordinary civilities and behaviour towards all men, did not only appear the fittest person the King could have chosen for that office in that time, but rendered himself so acceptable to all degrees of men that none but such who were implacable towards all who had ever disserved the King were sorry to see him promoted."[a] Notices and anecdotes of Manchester in his capacity of Lord Chamberlain to Charles II., and in other posts of dignity held by him towards the close of his life, are to be collected from the memoirs of the period. He died at Whitehall, May 5, 1671, at the age of sixty-eight years. He had been five times married. The present ducal house of Manchester is descended from the second marriage.

[a] Clarendon, ed. 1843, p. 1,005 (*Life*).

ERRATA IN DOCUMENTS.

Pp. 48, 49, 50, 52: for the signature "W. Jhonston" in these pages, read "A. Jhonston." He was the Scottish Commissioner, Sir Archibald Johnston, of Warriston; and the mistake has arisen from the peculiar shape of "A" in the copy of his signature.

P. 60, the sentence should stop after "Yorke" in line 3, and the words from "In the aforesaid" to "Lincolne" should run into one sentence with the following words, "the sinister endes," &c.

P. 61, line 7 from bottom, for "*Montagne's*" read "*Montague's*."

P. 63, last footnote, for "Rushwood" read "Rushworth."

P. 64, line 4, for "lefte on seconded" read "lefte onseconded;" which is a Scottish form for "left unseconded."

OLIVER CROMWELL

AND

THE EARL OF MANCHESTER.

No. 1.—For the Committee of both Kingdomes, &c.

My Lords and Gentlemen,
    The great necessities that the Scoch army and mine were in hath caused us to devide our armies, and to march into fresh quarters. I am upon my marche, and doe hope, God willing, to be at Doncaster to-morrow night, and there to stay untill I shall reseive your comands. My men, through want of clothes and other necessaries, fall sicke dayly. I hope the Lord will preserve us from any pestientiall disease, yet the Scoch army and mine is very much weakened through sicknes. I thinke fitt to give your Lo^{ps} an account where our quarters are. The Scotts are quartered at Leeds and Wakefield. I am quartered at Doncaster, and soe forward towards Newarke. Wee have left the Lord Fairefax with his forces in Yorke, and he hath now only some few castles that make oposition to him. My Lords, I shall not give you further trouble at this tyme then by offering the service of
    Your Lo^{ps} humble servant,
        MANCHESTER.
Fery brig, 22 July, 1644.

CAMD. SOC.   B

No. 2.—For the Committee of both Kingdomes, sitting at Derby House.

My Lords and Gentlemen,

Since my comeing to this place I have intended, as much as in mee lyes, the freeing of these parts from the violence and oppressions which they suffered under the garrisons of the enemy. Tychill Castle being the nerest and the most prejudiciall to the Isle of Axholme, I summoned at my first coming, and sent into the towne three hundred dragoones. Whereupon those of the place desired a parley, and have rendred the place unto mee. I have taken some 120 armes, some 80 horse, and have given libertie to the gentlemen to goe unto their severall dwellings, because they referred themselves very much to my disposall. The place is of consequence, in respect it lyes to hinder all commerce betwixt Derbyshire and these parts. I have sent to the Lord Fairfax to give him an accompt of it, that he may dispose of it as he pleases. I have nothing further to offer up unto your Lo^{ps} but to let you know that I waite your commands here, and shall be ready to obey them as

Your Lo^{ps} humble servant,

MANCHESTER.

Doncaster, 27th July, 1644.

No. 3.—For the Right Honourable the Committee of both Kingdomes, &c.

My Lords and Gentlemen,

Upon the receipt of your lettre of the 25th of July, the Earle of Leven, the Lord Fairefax and my selfe, with all the other chiefe officers belonging to our armies, had a consultacion what was fittest to be done upon the consideracion of your Lo^{ps} lettre. Wee found by our owne certaine intelligence that your Lo^{ps} informacion concerning Prince Rupert's being in Lancashire was not such as wee could rely upon; for the Prince, with all his best horse that he had remaining, quitted Lancashire upon Wednesday was senight, and past over into Cheshire at Hale Foard. His dragooners and such remainder of foote as he hath are dayly boated over from Leverpoole into Cheshire; the rest of his horse under the comand of Goreing, together with some foote under Col. Clavering, the Earle of Montrosse, are marched towards Cumberland and Westmoreland, soe as Lancashire have onely some petty garrisons left, which the forces in the county, if well imployed, may easily master. Wee therefore thought fitt thus to devide our forces, that I should march southward, and that the Scotts with their army should march for the security of those northerne counties, and to intend the takeing in of New Castle. Upon the takeing of this resolucion, I intend (God willing) to be my selfe at Lincolne by Satterday night, and shall intend the recruiting and refreshing of my forces with what speed I can, and I shall attend your Lo^{ps} commands which way you will have mee to march, and what you will have mee to doe. I shall humbly offer this unto your Lo^{ps}. I have sent to the Committee at Cambridge and the Committees of the sevrall counties to desire them that they would speed away recruites for this army, both of horse and foote. They returne mee this answere, that they have lately received an Ordinaunce of Parliament injoyning them to rayse a new force of horse, foote, and dragoones, which they are preparing to observe, and therefore doe desire mee to excuse them in that they are not able to doe, for they cannot pay nor recruite this army and raise such other forces as are required by that ordinance. I shall therefore desire to know which way your Lo^{ps} please to have those forces disposed, and I shall readily obey your orders, for it doth much frustrate my desires in doeing my duty at this time to want those recruites and supplyes which I thought to have found ready. But I submit all to your Lo^{ps} better judgments, onely I shall desire to cleere one thing which I heare is very confidently insisted upon, which is, that this army is really and fully payd. I shall as confidently affirme unto you that they are at this tyme in arreare since the first of January, upon halfe pay three monethes. The arreares before the first of January is more then since; and the Treasurers, which are two gentlemen of good creditt and esteeme, doe assure mee that within these few dayes there was yet unpaid 30,000$l.$ of the former three monethes assessments; of these last foure monethes, which is almost illapsed, there is nothing as yet brought in. I must confesse, and I doe acknowledge it as a blessing from God, that both the officers and soldiers have never yet refused any marching or duty for want of pay, and I hope they never will. It is therefore some trouble unto mee to see their necessities, and yet to heare the confidence of some affirmations that wee are payd to a day. My Lords, this I write that I may cleerly give you the truth, not that I will plead to be exempted from any duty or service that you shall command mee, for I am ready with that force I have (which yet I hope may doe you some service) to obey your orders as,

My Lords and Gentlemen, your Lo^{ps} most humble servant,

MANCHESTER.

Bloyth, 1° Augusti, 1644.

Since my comeing to Bloyth I heare there is two regiments of horse come into Newarke from Prince Rupert, with the assurance that the Prince will send some foote thether with all speed, but I hope neither his horse or foote shall doe any hurt to that county. I shall make the more hast into it.

No. 4.—To THE EARLE OF MANCHESTER.

MY LORD,

Wee have taken into consideracion the necessitie of hindering the recruites of Prince Rupert, and wholly to breake his army, if it bee possible. And to that end wee desire you to gather what force you can together forthwith. And with them, together with the forces of Nottinghamshire, Derbyshire, and Lancashire, as also those of Sir William Brereton and Sir Thomas Middleton, to all of which wee have written to that purpose, and to receive your orders to march toward Prince Rupert, and attend his motions, and follow him which way soever hee shall goe, and to take all advantages against him that shall bee offered. As to the money that is behind from the Associacion, wee have written to the several countyes, that with all expedition it may bee sent unto you wherever you shall bee, and have also appointed it to bee reported to the House that they will also use meanes to the countyes for expediteing thereof. Wee have your recruites in present consideracion, and hope to give you good satisfaccion concerning it, and that the ordinance shall be rather to the advantage thereof than other, and for Lincolneshire it is without the ordinance, and your Lo^p may doe there what you thinke fitt.

Gather your forces together.
Derbyshire, Nottinghamshire. Sir W. Brereton and Sir Tho. Middleton to joyne and receive orders.

Counties written to for your money.

Your recruites in consideration.

Lincolneshire not in the Ordinance.

Signed, &c.
W. SAY AND SEALE.   JO. MAITLAND.

Derby House, 6° Augusti, 1644.

Sent by Mr. Potter att night.

NO. 5.—FOR THE RIGHT HONOURABLE THE COMMITTEE OF BOTH KINGDOMES.

MY LORDS AND GENTLEMEN,

In my march from Yorke towards Lincolne I was earnestly intreated, by divers in those parts of Yorkeshire about Sheffield, that I would consider of the great spoyle that the guarrison in Sheffield did unto the places neere adjoyning, and likewise of the consequence of the place in regard of the great comoditie of iron wares that were vented there. I was further moved by the Committee and gentlemen of Nottingham for the reduceing of the guarrison in Welbeck to the obedience of Parliament, because it was a great anoyance to those parts. Whereupon I resolved to goe myselfe with a great part of my forces to Welbecke, and to send Generall Major Crawford with the rest unto Sheffcild. Upon my comeing neere Welbecke, I sent in a summons to the place, and they, with great civillity, sent to parley with mee; and the next day being Friday they rendred the house unto mee upon composicion. I was willing to give them the larger termes, because I was not in a condition to beseidge a place soe well fortified as that was; and therefore I gave the officers and soldiers liberty to march with all their armes, colours flying, and other pontillions of warr. But when I came to take possession of the house, most of all the soldiers came unto mee to lay downe their armes, and would not carry them, but desired ticketts of mee to goe to their owne homes, the which I graunted them, soe as I had 350 musquetts in the house, 50[tie] horse armes, 11 peeces of canon, great and small, whereof one the governor had libertie to carry away. I had likewise 20[tie] barrells of powder and a tonne of match. The house I preserved entire, and have put a guarrison into it of Nottinghamshire men untill I know your Lo[ps] resolucions, whether you will have it slighted or not. The place is very regularly fortified, and the Marquesse of Newcastle's daughters and the rest of his children and family are in it, unto whome I have engaged myselfe for their quiet aboade there, and to intercede to the Parliament for a compleate maintenance for them. In the which I shall beseech your Lordships that they may have your favour and furtherance. I am now my selfe come to Lincolne, and those forces that were with mee I have quartered about Gainsborough and those places, that I may give them some refreshing after the great hardship they have endured. And I expected here to have found the recruets for this army, according to the often and earnest lettres that I have written unto the Committees of these associated counties. But all

the returne I have is your Lo^{ps} lettres pressing them to raise and set forth a new force both of horse and foote under other comanders, which it seemes are already chosen. This puts me into an unserviceable condicion, and therefore I desire to know what your Lo^{ps} intencions are in the disposeing of these forces, and I shall readily obey your comands. If your Lo^{ps} please to have me to deliver over the remainder of this force I now have into the hands of those collonells and captains that are to be chosen to give a supplie to that army that is now to be raised, I shall very readily obey your order. If your Lo^{ps} intencions be to dispose of these forces otherwise, I shall with all care observe your comands as
      Your Lo^{ps} humble servant,
          MANCHESTER.
Lincolne, August 6th, 1644.

No. 6.—To my Lord of Manchester.

MY LORD,

In the close of our last wee assured your Lo^p that wee would have care of your recreutes, and that wee hoped the new Ordinance should rather bee to the advantage of your recreuts than otherwise. Accordingly wee have reported it the Houses, who have agreed that 1800 foot bee sent for the recruiting of your army out of the forces to bee levied upon the new Ordinance within the Association. *1800 foot for your recruit.*
   Signed, &c.
     W. SAY AND SEALE. JO. MAITLAND.

Derby House, 7° Augusti, 1644.

By the Post.

8   CROMWELL AND THE EARL OF MANCHESTER.

No. 7.—To THE EARLE OF MANCHESTER.

MY LORD,

Orders of the House appoint you 1800 foot for your recruit.

Wee sent unto you yesterday the Orders of the Houses appointing 1800 foot for recreuting of your forces out of the forces of your Association now levying upon the new Ordinance. Wee have received lettres from the Committee of Essex, desireing the recruites required of them by you to bee respited for some tyme, till the forces they are now levying bee first raised. Wee doe therefore desire your Lo^p to take noe more recruites from them than necessity shall require, because that an entire formed regiment of 1000 is to bee raysed out of that county upon the new Ordinance.

1000 to bee raised in Essex.

Signed, &c.

W. SAY AND SEALE.   JO. MAITLAND.

Darby House, 9° Augusti, 1644.

By Rowland Fankerd, about two afternoone.

No. 8.—FOR THE RIGHT HONOURABLE THE COMMITTEE OF BOTH KINGDOMES, SITTING AT DARBY HOUSE.

MY LORDS AND GENTLEMEN,

I received your Lo^{ps} lettre yesterday, by which your comands were that I should gather what force I could and march towards Prince Rupert, and to attend his mocions and follow him which way soever he shall goe. This appeared to me so large a comission, and a worke so difficult, considering the weake condicion of the forces that are here with mee, who are now under great indisposicions and infeccions, as that upon the receipt of your Lo^{ps} order and comand I called together such of my chiefe officers as were here with mee to consult which way I might serve your Lo^{ps} according to your comands. And from them I received this inclosed paper, which I take the boldnes to offer to your Lo^{ps}, as the result of our debate here, which I doubt not but will carry more weight and receive the better acceptacion, because it is not a single opinion. My Lords and Gentlemen, these I tender to you in dutie, and submit them to your better judgments, and beseech you to believe that I doe not dispute your comands, but only give you a true accompt of my condicion, and shall observe what further you shall comand mee, as

Your humble servant,
MANCHESTER.

Lincolne, 10º Aug. 1644.

Consideracions concerning the marching of the Earl of Manchester's army into Cheshire.

1. By marching thither, as is required, it cannot be expected wee should force Prince Rupert to a second ingagement in the field this summer, neither (considering the posture he lies in about Chester, and the opertunity of shifting his horse through Chester from one side of the river Dee to the other, whereof he possesses all the passes for twentie miles upwards from Chester, and below there are none at all) is it likely that we can force his horse to quitt their quarters about Chester and goe away. If we could doe soe, should we draw away presently, they might returne; should we follow them with our horse through Wales, or where ever they goe, it would be a surer way to ruine our horse then the enemies.

To beseidge Chester is not a worke for one moneth in the latter end of a summer, neither is it likely wee shall gather there a sufficient force (free from other ingagements) suddenly to doe it, the worke requiring as great a force as the seige of Yorke, or greater.

The end, therefore, and busines intended, we suppose, will be to lye with a comanding body of horse near Chester, to hinder Rupert from raising any new force in those parts, or receiving any accession of such as would come or be sent from other parts of this Kingdome (for from Ireland we cannot hinder any whilest they have all the ports on their side), and either this or the seiging of Chester would necessarily keepe us there all winter.

2. If then wee should goe farr of to soe long a worke, wee must either take with us sufficiencie of force and all stores and accomodacions to serve us for the whole tyme, as to need noe supplyes while we are like to stay, or we must provide for a certain way of all supplyes to come unto us. For the first we cannot goe so provided, being in present great want of ammunicion and equipage of all sorts for the traine, but especially of match (our supplyes thereof sent for by sea being lately taken by the enemie); our regiments in great need of recreuts, especially our foote, and of the men wee have both horse and foote (by the former hardships suffered) soe many sick and wounded, and more dayly falling sicke, as if we should now march wee must leave a third part behind us; our arrears of pay intollerable (our horse having had little or none since the 25th March, which hath cast them into extreame want of all necessaryes); neither have we money in tresurie to take with us for better encouragements in the future. If we could goe soe well provided in all these respects for a long time, yet it were noe wisdome (depending thereon) to engage soe farr of, and not provided for a way of new supplyes, if we should happen to want before that worke were done.

For the second, therefore (the securing of a way for our supplyes), there being noe possibility of any comeing to us by sea on that side of the kingdome, nor by any navigable river in our power, all supplyes and recruets we should want (of men, horses, armes, ammunicion, tresury, or any thing) must come to us by land from this side the kingdome, and passe under the danger of Belvoyr and Newarke, and of Bolsover and Tidbury Castles (if the nearest way from those parts), or of other enemy[s] guarrisons, if any other way about.

3. Upon all these consideracions, therefore, it cannot be fit to goe with this army into Cheshire unlesse (at least) those four guarrisons were first taken, or provision made by a sufficient force to blocke them up or insconse them.

Neither indeed can this army soe well march hence any way without providing against Newarke, least that active and politicke enemy (having already got together againe a body of 800 horse with Hastings his horse, who joyne continually to serve each others turnes, and are even now continually during to attempt or annoy our horse quarters) doe (if they have scope left to range) over runne these partes againe, weaken, if not destroy, our guarrisons, greaten themselves, and gather fresh force against the spring. This is easie to forsee and twice taught by experience when they have bin weaker then now, and our Lincolnshire and Nottinghamshire forces stronger. Whereas, these fierie enemyes guarrisons being taken and blocked up, it will gaine unto the Parliament the advantage of raiseing new forces, and maintenance for them, out of five or six counties thereby cleared, which have hitherto beene soe infested as we could never yet by all our garrisons in them, either raise any force considerable in them, or support what they have had. And this done will render also most of our guarrisons in these partes needlesse, or able to spare the greatest part of their present strength into field service.

4. To this soe necessary a worke (and without which first provided for we cannot goe to stay and doe the busines in those westerne partes) this army will not suffice, and spare any foote at all to march thither as is required, our foote, sicke and sound, being not above 6000.

5. This army may doe that worke of these parts, and both keepe its selfe entire, and lye fitly the while to receive our recreuts and supplyes needful, and ready also to secure and further serve the Associacion and southern partes upon occasion.

6. The Associacion by which wee were raised and should be payd (as they have been already much discontented at our drawing soe

farr into the North, and leaving them naked; see if wee shall now again draw off soe farre westward and leave them soe long without the protection for which wee were designed, and Newark, Belvoir, &c. at liberty to infest them with incursions) will have just cause to withdraw or slacken their hands from our further recreuting or maintenance, and seeke for some other body and head to protect them, and the same only to be maintained by them.

No. 9.—To the Earle of Manchester.

My Lord,

Your Lo^{ps} of the 6th present from Lincolne wee have received, conteyning your takeing in of Welbeck house. Wee congratulate with your Lo^p that good successse which God is pleased still to give to your endeavours, and doe approve your Lo^{ps} termes granted them, as whereby your Lo^p have not only gained the house but the men also, as appeares by their voluntary render of their armes. And wee shall give all furtherance to your Lo^{rs} desire to the houses for makeing good your engagements to them. As to your Lo^{ps} recreuts mentioned, wee are sorry they were not ready to attend your order; yet wee are assured you shall have a better account of them than those lettres. And wee hope before this tyme our letters are come to your hands, whereby you will discerne that the Ordinance of the 12th of July shall be noe disadvantage to your forces; for, besides that 1,800 of those are ordered for your recreuts, your Lo^p may doe as you please in Lincolneshire, which is not within the Ordinance. And besides the countye have assured us that they are about those levyes for your Lo^p; however, by those letters they would represent their difficulties to see if they could gett any ease, especially this harvest tyme. And wee desire your Lo^p to beleive that it was not the intention of the Houses to doe any thing in that Ordinance that should in any sort prejudice your army, which,

Welbeck House taken in.

The souldiers voluntarily render their armes.

Ordinance of July the 12th noe hindrance to your recreuts. Lincolneshire not within the Ordinance.

under your conduct, by the blessing of God, hath beene soe prosperous and serviceable to the whole Kingdome, and of which, by the same blessing, wee have reason to hope for the same good service and successe for the future.

Signed, &c.

Darby House, 13° Augusti, 1644.

By Col. Fleetwood, who went the 15th instant.

No. 10.—For the Committee of both Kingdomes sitting at Derby House, &c.

My Lords and Gentlemen,

I received your Lop^{ps} letter of the 9th of August, signifying your pleasure that I shall take noe more recreutes from the county of Essex then necessity shall require, because an intire regiment of 1000 is to be raysed in that county. I shall obey your Lo^{ps} comands, only I thinke fit to acquaint your Lo^{ps} what order I had formerly setled for the recreute of these forces. Those countyes out of which the regimentes were at first raised I had appointed to supply the defectes of such regimentes as were by them raised, and I found this way to give the best satisfaction to the counties, and made the soldiers more united among themselves. My owne regimente being raised in Essex, I thought to have recreuted it from thence, it being much weakened through some service it hath done, and by reason of sicknes that is amongst them. Yet, your Lo^{ps} having otherwise ordered it, I shall rather runne the hazard of other inconveniences which I feare then give a checke to your other designes.

My Lords and Gentlemen,

I am your Lo^{ps} most humble servant,

MANCHESTER.

Lincolne, 14th August, 1644.

No. 11.—To the Earle of Manchester.

My Lord,

The state of Prince Rupert's army being other than hee conceived when wee wrote last unto you, there being soe many of his forces marched northward, together with the consideration of your Lo^{ps} lettre ; and the reasons inclosed have caused us to alter our resolution, and to desire that your Lo^p will send such a party as you shall thinke fitt, to joyne with the forces in our former lettres expressed to bee sent from Nottinghamshire, Derbyshire, Lancashire, Cheshire, and Sir Thomas Middleton, and to make what improvement may bee of those joyned forces to hinder his recreuts, and to proceed further as there shall bee occasion and opertunitie offered. The rest of your forces may stay where you thinke fittest for their recreuts from the Association, and for further service. In the meane tyme wee desire you to keepe constant intelligence both with the Scottish army and with the Lord Fairfax, that you may bee ready for the assistance of Yorkshire, if the forces that are in Westmorland and Cumberland should againe fall into those parts. And wee desire also that your Lo^p will send one thousand foot to Abbington with all speed.

Send a party to hinder Prince Rupert's recruites.

Rest of your forces to stay where you thinke fittest for their recruits.

Keepe intelligence with the Scottish and Lo. Fairfax his army.

Send 1000 foot to Abbington.

Signed, &c.

W. Say and Seale.   Jo. Maitland.

Derby House, 14° Augusti, 1644.

By Col. Fleetwood.

No. 12.—To the Earle of Manchester.

My Lord,

The forces of Hartfordshire levied upon the new Ordinance having received order from us to march to Abbington have this

morning sent us word that they are upon their march; therefore, wee desire your Lo^p that they may bee part of that 1000 which your Lo^p was to send thither. Your Lo^p may please to appoint over them such a major as you shall thinke fitt, or to imbody them with other forces to make them a regiment. And for the forces of Norfolke or Suffolke, the disposition of the major being by the Ordinance left to this Committee, wee desire your Lo^p to appoint over them whom you please. But for the Major of Essex, att the instant request of the Committee of that county, wee have bestowed it upon Major Moore. And for the supplying of the rest of your 1000 wee have appointed that Colonell Ayloff's men now att Newport shall march thither, which with 200 of your men att Aylesbury shall make up that number which wee desired for Abbington, which wee conceived most convenient in respect of their neerenesse to the rendeyvous, and that thereby there will bee none drawne from your Lo^{ps} army. Wee have just now received the newes (by a lettre from your Lo^{ps} Scout-mastr to Doctor Stomes) of the takeing of Sheffield Castle. Wee blesse God for your good successe, and give your Lo^p thankes for that good service.

Hertfordshire levies to bee part of 1000 men for Abbington.

Col. Ayloff's and 200 of yours at Aylesbury to make upp the 1000.

        Signed, &c.
          W. Say and Seale.   Jo. Maitland.

Derby House, 15° Augusti, 1644.

    By Colonell Fleetwood.

No. 13.—To the Earle of Manchester.

My Lord,

Wee have received from the gentlemen of Yorkshire here in towne the proposition which wee send herewith inclosed, and doe recommend it and the state of that county to your Lo^p, and desire

Yorkeshire commended to your Lo^{ps} care.

that by intelligence held with the Earle of Leven and the Lord Fairfax (to whom wee have written in like manner) such course may bee taken therein as to you (who are nearer the place) shall seeme fitt.

    Signed, &c.
      W. SAY AND SEALE.   JO. MAITLAND.

Derby House, 21° Augusti, 1644.

 By the post att night.

No. 14.—FOR THE COMMITTEE OF BOTH KINGDOMES.

I have received your lettres by Maister Harrison, and returne your Lo^{ps} many humble thanks for the notice you were pleased to take of those services which have been lately done by the forces under my command. I shall desire to doe my uttmost in discharge of that trust the Parliament hath beene pleased to honour mee with, and I trust that God will blesse the endeavours of your servantes. This day I recieved advertisement from my forces that lyes before Wingfield Manner, that that place is rendred unto them upon composition, soe as I hope I shall now have all my forces together to refresh and recreute them, and be ready for any further service your Lo^{ps} shall comand. In obedience to these last lettres, I shall prepare a party to send into Cheshire. But, before I send them away, I shall consult with the Committees of Derby and Nottingham, to know what assistance they will give, their countryes being now free by the takeing of these guarrisons. I shall from tyme to tyme give your Lo^{ps} an account of the occurency of these parts, and be always ready to obey all your comands as,

    My Lords and Gentlemen,
      Your Lo^{ps} most humble servant,
        MANCHESTER.

Lincolne, 21th Aug. 1644.

No. 15—To the Earle of Manchester.

My Lord,

Sir William Waller takes all his forces speedily from Abbington, and goes westward for my Lord Generall's assistance. Sir Charles Gerard and Sir Baynam Throgmorton (as wee heare) is come out of Wales with his forces on this side Bath. Sir Francis Dorrington hath a thousand horse. When Sir William Waller is past them, they may joyne and bee able to levie men to raise the seige at Basing, and to remove the Parliament forces now att Abbington, any of which will bee of very ill consequence. Wee have therefore written to the Committee in Essex to send their new regiment to Abbington, understanding from them that as yet they had noe direction from your Lo^{pp}. These and your other forces are there as part of your army, and to bee joyned with it when this emergent necessitie is over. Wee hope God will soe prosper our affaires in the north that your Lo^p may come with your army neare Oxford, and then this regiment will bee in a readines for you, and in the meane tyme kept from a long march backward and forward.

Sir W. Waller marcheth westward.

Sir Charles Gerard and Dorrington may joyne.

Essex regiment ordered to march to Abbington.

Derby House, 22° Augusti, 1644.

By the Post.

No. 16.—To the Earle of Manchester.

My Lord,

Wee wrote unto your Lo^p formerly that wee had given order to the Committee of Essex to march to Abbington with their new regiment, the forces of Sir W. Waller being to remove from thence speedily, and to bee employed in the west for the assistance of my Lord Generall. This day wee have received a lettre from that

Committee desireing more cleerly to understand our orders, to whom wee have written that our intentions were that they should march both horse and foot to Abbington, wherewith wee thought fitt likewise to acquaint your Lo^p. Wee have also given order to 300 of the Hartfordshire forces to march to Abbington, and the remaining two hundred to march to Aylesbury to supply the absence of Lieutenant-Colonel Sadler's forces, whom wee have sent to Abbington.

Signed, &c.

TH. WHARTON.   JO. MAITLAND.

Derby House, 24° Aug. 1644.

By Rowland Fankerd att ten att night.

No. 17.—FOR THE COMMITTEE OF BOTH KINGDOMES, SITTING AT DERBY HOUSE.

MY LORDS AND GENTLEMEN,

According to your comand I prepared a considerable party of horse and dragoones to send into Cheshire, and consulted with the Nottingham and Derby Committees what numbers they could aford in conjuncture with those whom I should send, but I find that they are not able to give any assistance at all. I find likewise, by lettres from Sir John Meldrum, that the Lancashire forces, being a very great body, and having done very considerable services lately in routing the forces of the enemy, are not willing to come out of their owne country. I have received this day intelligence, both by lettres from Sir William Brereton and others, that Prince Rupert is marching southward. Of these things I thought fitt to give your Lo^{ps} an account, and to knowe your further pleasure, whether you will have those horse which I send, to march into Cheshire, notwithstanding these advertisements, and that there can

be noe assistance expected from Derby and Nottingham. Whatsoever your Lo^ps shall further comand shall be obeyed by
    Your Lo^ps most humble servant,
                MANCHESTER.
Lincolne, 26th Aug. 1644.

No. 18.—FOR THE COMMITTEE OF BOTH KINGDOMES, &c.

MY LORDS AND GENTLEMEN,
    I have received your lettre which mentions your comanding the Essex forces to march to Abbington. All your comandes are very willingly obeyed by mee. I have likewise received a lettre from your Lo^ps with some proposicions that were tendred to you from the Yorkeshire gentlemen concerning the raysing of more forces in that county. I thinke it a very fitt thing, and gave my advice to the Lord Fairfax at my first comeing into those partes that it was of absolute necessity to raise a good strength. I am certaine the condicion of those partes are such as they have not only oportunity to raise men, but alsoe meanes to defray the charge. I shall not further trouble your Lo^ps at this tyme, but rest,
        My Lords and Gentlemen,
            Your Lo^ps most humble servant,
                MANCHESTER.
Lincolne, 27 Aug. 1644.

No. 19.—TO THE EARLE OF MANCHESTER.

MY LORD,
    Wee have here inclosed sent to your Lo^p the informations wee have this day received from Lancashire and Cheshire. Wee doubt not but according to our former direction you have sent a party to joyne with Sir John Meldrum and Sir William Brereton and to

Wee doubt not a party sent to Sir John Meldrum and Sir WilliamBrereton.

20 CROMWELL AND THE EARL OF MANCHESTER.

suppresse the forces with Prince Rupert by the [aid[1]] of the forces from Westmoreland. Wee recomend to your especiall care that such a party may bee forthwith sent as may prevent this great and growing mischeife, and that your Lo^p would carefully observe the desires in our former letters sent to you concerning Prince Rupert's army.

Derby House, 27° Augusti, 1644.

By the Post.

No. 20.—To the Earle of Manchester.

Copies to your Lo^p of Lord Generall Sir W. Waller and Col Middleton's.

Prince Rupert marched south; joyned with Westmorland party; is considerable.

To march with your whole army upp to Woodstocke.

Ready to assist our forces in the West.

If Rupert's horse onely march, then lett your horse march and foote follow.

Wee have herewith sent you copies of our lettres from my Lord Generall Sir W. Waller and Collonel Middleton, whereby your Lo^p will understand the condition of our affaires in the West. By your lettres of the 26th of this instant wee perceive your intelligence is that Prince Rupert with his force is marching southward, with which our informations doe concurre, and that, the Lancashire and Westmoreland horse being joyned with him, hee is a considerable body, which may distresse the party with Colonel Middleton, and by calling off that party will in probability ruine the army with my Lord Generall. Wee therefore, upon serious debate, conceive it most necessary if Prince Rupert do march upwards, that your Lo^p with your whole army doe march towards Woodstocke, which wee conceive the readiest way to assist our forces in the West, but wee leave it unto your Lo^p; and wee earnestly desire you that notwithstanding any seige or recreute you would (leaving sufficient forces to secure your association) with speed march accordingly. But if Prince Rupert come upp with his horse onely, wee desire your horse may forthwith goe on and your foote follow, because in probability the tyme of releife of the party with Coll. Middleton

[1] Blank in MS.

and my Lord Generall's army will bee past before your foote can come upp. But if upon good intelligence your Lo^{pp} doe find that Prince Rupert with his forces doe not march upwards, wee desire your Lo^{pp} will then send a considerable party to joyne with the Cheshire and other forces. And for the other part of your army, besides the party sent into Cheshire and those left to secure your association, wee offer this to your consideration, that your Lo^p with the rest of your forces will speedily come upp to Abbington where two of your regiments will bee, in which parts wee very much want forces for the publique good; and where your forces may doe very great service and your recruites goe on. For this last particular if you approve of it wee desire you speedily to putt itt into execution; if not, wee desire speedily to heare from you.

Derby House, 28° Aug. 1644.

By Gardner.

No. 21.—To the Earle of Manchester.

My Lord,

Upon information given us that Sir John Norwich and the horse under his command had beene for a long tyme out of any employment, wee sent for him to this Committee, and gave him orders to march to Abbington; but, being informed by him that his horse was a part of your Lo^{ps} army, wee altered our resolutions, and ordered him with all expedition to march to your Lo^{pp}, which hee accepted very willingly and promised to performe. It is now above a moneth since hee received our orders, and wee doe not understand as yet that hee hath putt them in execution. We doe therefore desire your Lo^p to command him speedily to repaire unto your army, and obey such orders as hee shall receive from your Lo^p, which, if hee shall neglect to doe, wee desire your Lo^{pp} to cashiere him of his charge, and to take such course as you shall thinke fitt to secure the horse under his command, and their armes for the service of the State.

     Signed, &c.
       NORTHUMBERLAND.   JO. MAITLAND.
Derby House, 29 Augusti, 1644.

By Rouland Fankeard.

No. 22.—To the Earle of Manchester.

My Lord,

Necessity of your march westward.   By the enclosed copie of my Lord Generall's letter your Lo^p will see the state of our affaires in the west, and the necessity of your speedy march that way with all the forces you can, according to our former orders. Wee desire you with all expedition to bend your course that way, and wee hope there will bee such union and agreement among yourselves, and all differences soe composed and forgotten, as shall enable them to prosecute the warre effectually to an happy and speedy end. Wee have given order to the rest of our forces to come to a rendez-vous for the joynt prosecution of the warre.

     Signed, &c.
Derby House, 1° Septembris, 1644.

By John Arnold att five att night, and a duplicate of this by Mr. Binding att eleven att night.

No. 23.—To the Earle of Manchester.

My Lord,

 Wee have received informacion that the forces that were with *Prince Rupert marched toward Bristoll.* Prince Rupert are marched toward Bristoll. Wee therefore desire your Lo^{pp} to send all the horse you can spare with all expedition

to Abbington (leaving onely soe many as may serve to march upp with your foot), with which, and the rest of your horses, wee desire you will also march according to our former orders. And for those forces that are gone toward Cheshire, wee desire (seeing the forces that lately fought with Sir William Brereton's are marched away) that you will give order to them to march the nearest way forthwith to Abbington. *Send all the horse you can spare to Abbington.*
    Signed, &c.
    NORTHUMBERLAND.   JO. MAITLAND.
Derby House, 2° Septembris, 1644.

One by Mr. Potter, another by the Post, third by R. Fankeard on Tuesday att night September the *How and when sent.*

No. 24.—For the Committee of both Kingdomes, &c.

My Lords and Gentlemen,

I have received your lettre of the 29 of Aug. and shall observe your comands in marching towards you as soone as I can. I had designed a party of horse and dragoones for Cheshire, and they were 20 miles onward of their march. But receiving lettres from Sir William Brereton which doe assure me of the Prince's being gone out of those parts, and his horse and foote gotten very neare Bristoll by the way of Wales, I have recalled my horse and dragoones, and intend to march with all the force I have to Abbington. I shall from tyme to tyme give your Lo^{pps} an account of my marches, and shall obey your Lo^{ps} comands as
    Your Lo^{ps} most humble servant,
        MANCHESTER.
Lincolne, 2° Sept. 1644.

No. 25.—For the Committee of both Kingdomes, &c.

My Lords and Gentlemen,

I have received your lettre of the second of September, and likewise the duplicate thereof. I shall obey your comands, and am now upon my march. As soone as I can get some money, which I have sent for, and expect it to morrow night or Thursday, I shall then send away before me to Abbington as many of the horse as shall be judged convenient to be spared from the foote, and, with the rest of the horse and foote, I shall make what haste I can to Abbington according to your comandes. I am,
My Lords and Gentlemen,
Your most humble servant,
Manchester.

Lincolne, 4° Sept. 1644.

No. 26.—For the Committee of both Kingdomes, &c.

My Lords and Gentlemen,

I have received your Lo^{ps} lettre of the third of this instant and am making what hast possibly I can to obey your comands. I quarter this night at Bowrne, and shall have, God willing, all those forces of horse and foote to morrow night quartered at Peterborough or Stamford, and soe to Huntington; for it is of absolute necessity wee march that way in regard of money and other necessaryes which wee want and hope to be supplied of them there. I intend, God willing, to be at Huntington to-morrow night my selfe to get in readinesse all things that shall be wanting for the horse, that I may send them away before the foote, and shall march away with

the foote and the rest of the horse as fast as possibly I can to Abbington. My Lords and Gentlemen I shall be always ready to observe your comands as,
                    Your Lo^{ps} most humble servant,
                                        MANCHESTER.
Bonrne, 5° Sept. 1644.

No. 27.—FOR THE COMMITTEE OF BOTH KINGDOMES, &c.

MY LORDS AND GENTLEMEN,

I received this morning your Lo^{ps} lettre, together with a copy of my Lord Generall's lettre, which gives a very sad account of his present condition, of the which I have a very deepe sense. The Lord's arme is not shortned though wee be much weakned. I trust he will gives us a happy recovery. I shall, with all the speed I can, march in observance of your former orders. I cannot expect to have any recreutes, being I am to march soe sudden from these partes, which will be a great disappointing to me considering the weakenes of these forces. I shall from tyme to tyme acquaint your Lo^{ps} with my marches. Concerning those differences which your Lo^{ps} take notice to be amongst some of this army, I hope your Lo^{ps} shall finde that I shall take such care as, by the blessing of God, nothing of the publique service shall be retarded.
        My Lords and Gentlemen, I am
                    Your Lo^{ps} most humble servant,
                                        MANCHESTER.
Huntington, Sept. 8°, 1644.

No. 28.—TO THE EARLE OF MANCHESTER.

MY LORD,

Counties written too to hasten your recruites.

Wee have written to all the countyes of your Association to speed away the remainder of the forces assigned to your Lo^{pp} for recreuts, or otherwise; a copie whereof wee send inclosed, and desire your

Appoint some officers to conduct them.

Lo^{pp} to give your orders accordingly, and appoint some officers to conduct them to your Lo^{pp}, and not retard your march.

Signed, &c.

Derby House, 9° September, 1644.

By John Preistly.

No. 29.—TO MY LORD OF MANCHESTER.

MY LORD,

Wee have received agayne this day intelligence that the horse of my Lord Generall, under the command of Commissary Generall

Behre and Middleton joyned.

Behre, and those with Lieutenant-Generall Middleton, are joyned together, and are marching toward Somerton and Weymouth.

Foote on their way to Southampton.

And that the foote were all come as farre as Okehampton, towards Southampton, where there will bee both armes and cloathes for them, and wee hope there will bee speedily a very good army on

King intends for Oxford.

foote agayne. The King intends with his army to march to Oxford if he can get through. Therefore wee desire your Lo^{pp} to make all the expedition you can possible to Abbington, and to give us advertisement of your marches as you proceed.

Derby House, 11° 7bris. 1644.

By Binding att nine att night.

No. 30.—For the Committee of both Kingdomes.

My Lords and Gentlemen,
I have received your Lo[ps] lettre of the 21th of this instant, together with the votes of both Houses of Parliament, the which I shall readily obey. I am now upon my march to Reading according to your former orders. I have already written to Sir William Waller to give him an account where I intend to be according to your orders, and I shall from tyme to tyme keepe as an exact intelligence with him as I can. Your Lo[ps] shall not need to feare any disagreement on my part in point of comand. The only difficulty I looke upon (which I hope your Lo[ps] will take into your consideracion), that when wee doe joyne wee may have such a considerable strength as may keepe up the reputacion of an army.
My Lords and Gentlemen, I am
Your Lo[ps] humble servant,
MANCHESTER.

Watford, 22 Sept. 1644.

No. 31.—To the Earle of Manchester.

My Lord,
By the order enclosed your Lo[pp] will see the resolucion of the House of Commons concerning your march, and what they expect in reference to that order, which wee have therefore sent your Lo[pp], and doe most earnestly desire you that according to that order and our former requests your Lo[pp] will speed your march into the west. The enemies horse wee heare are come to Bridgwater, the foote to Crediton, and comeing eastward. Your Lo[pp] was present att our debates and doe know the necessitie of this service. Wee desire by

Speed your march into the West according to your order from the House.

the messenger to heare from you. The House of Commons will expect a dayly knowledge of your Lo^{ps} pursuing their desires.

Derby House, 24° Sept^{br}, 1644.

By Mr. Binding.

No. 32.—FOR THE RIGHT HONORABLE THE COMMITTEE OF BOTH KINGDOMES, &c.

MY LORDS AND GENTLEMEN,

I have received your Lo^{ps} lettre, together with the vote of the House of Commons. It is very probable that that House and your Lo^{ps} may be informed of my being at Uxbridg; for the bridge of Maydenhead being broken, I am constrayned to stay untill it be soe mended as that I may passe over; which my carpenters enformed me could not be done untill this night. This also being the fast day I thought it a duty to seeke God. Your Lo^{ps} may be assured that I shall march as soone as with any conveniency I can, and, therefore, I shall desire that favour from your Lo^{ps} that my former observances to your commands may somewhat prevaile in lessening the opinions of my backwardnesse to obey your comands. I was present at some of the debates which your Lo^{ps} mention, and your Lo^{ps} know what my humble opinion was. I am still of the same minde, that if the King be upon his march, in that condition that I see those armyes in, you doe expose us to scorne, if not to ruine; but, my Lords, when my sense is delivered I shall obey as farre as in me lyes. Your Lo^{ps} desire me to send my horse before me westward. Your Lo^{ps} know that you have comanded most of my horse and some foote and dragoones to Banbury. I have with me but a compleat number to guard the foote that are with me. Your Lo^{ps} shall have a dayly account of my pursuing your orders.

My Lords and Gentlemen, I am your humble servant,

MANCHESTER.

Harfeild, 25 Sept. 1644.

No. 33.—To the Earle of Manchester.

My Lord,

Wee received your lettre, and doe assure ourselves your Lo^{pp} will speedily march with your forces westward. But where your Lo^{pp} writes of this Committee's ordering most of your horse, some dragooners and foote, our orders were because of the forces of Prince Rupert about Evesholme, and the enemies entring your Association, that 1500 of your horse and dragoones should stay about Oxford; but how many dragoones was left to your pleasure, and out of which 1500 your Lo^{pp} might send some into Lincolne-shire soe they exceed not 500; and all the rest of your horse and foote were forthwith to march into the West, and your horse to goe on before your foote, excepting soo many horse as shall bee necessary to march with your foote.

<small>Our orders were in regard of Rupert att Evesholme. 1500 horse and dragoones to stay about Oxford. All the rest to march into the West.</small>

<small>Derby House, 26° Septembris, 1644.</small>

By John Preistly att eight att night and duplicate.

No. 34.—For the Right Honourable, &c.

My Lords and Gentlemen,

I have received your letter and shall with what I can obey your comands. I hope you will be carefull to hasten such forces as were in your intentions to send, for these that are with me are not a strength sufficient to hazard the issue of our affayres upon. This day most of my forces are to passe over at Maydenhead, which they could not have done sooner. I have sent 500 horse into Lincoln-shire. I have left Lieut.-Generall Cromwell's regiment of horse at

Banbury with 3 companyes of dragoones and 7 companyes of foote. The rest of the horse and foote are with mee. I am,
My Lords and Gentlemen,
Your Lo^{ps} most humble servant,
MANCHESTER.

Harfeild, 27 Sept. 1644.

No. 35.—TO THE EARLE OF MANCHESTER.

MY LORD,

Wee have received information from Lieutenant-Generall Cromwell that Sir Thomas Glemham with 21 col[ou]rs of horse and dragoones is marched from Newarke by Ashby, as it is beleived with an intention to raise the seige at Banbury or joyne with Prince Rupert. Wee have written to Colonell Fleetwood, if that information shall prove true, to returne with the 500 horse sent into Lincolneshire under his command, to such place as Lieutenant-Generall Cromwell shall appoint for his assistance against themselves. Wee wrote unto your Lo^p formerly to leave onely about Oxford 1,500 horse and dragoones, and with all the rest of your forces, horse and foot, to march westward, and to send your horse before your foot, leaving onely with your foot a sufficient guard. According to the order of the House of Commons, the copie whereof is here inclosed, wee againe desire your Lo^p to use all possible expedition in your march westward, and to send your horse before your foot, leaving onely with your foot a sufficient guard, which wee conceive five hundred to bee upon consideracion of the informations wee have received concerning the marching of the King's forces eastward, and of the waies and meanes to oppose their designes. Wee have thought fitt to write to Sir W. Waller that if the King's forces shall continue westward that hee stay about Shaftsbury, if hee can doe it with safety. And if the King shall march eastward,

Sir Thomas Glemham marched from Newarke.

If soe, Col. Fleetwood to returne out of Lincolneshire.

To leave 1500 horse and dragoones about Oxford.

Use all possible expedition in your march westward.

Sir. W. Waller to stay about Shaftsbury if the King stays westward.

that hee come to Marlborough or thereabouts, to which places my Lord Generall (according as hee shall heare of the King's motions) is to send 1,500 of his horse, or at least soe many as hee can have in readinesse; and wee doe likewise desire your Lo^p to send your horse (soe many as may guard your foote excepted) to the same places of Shaftsbury or Marlborough, according as you shall understand of the motions of the King's forces. Wee have desired my Lord Generall to send his foot to Newbury, to which place wee desire your Lo^p to cause your foot to march; and wee shall use our best endeavours to hasten thither the citty forces.

Send your forces to Shaftsbury or Marlborough.

Derby House, 28° Septembris, 1644.

By Mr. Butler.

No. 36.—For the Committee of both Kingdomes, &c.

My Lords and Gentlemen,

I am now at Reading, and have received letters from Sir William Waller by which he advertises mee of his being at Shaftsbury with a reasonable good body of horse and dragoones, but the foote which he had with him he hath beene inforced to divide into Plymouth and the port townes of those countyes, soe as he hath none or but few with him. I believe, therefore, your Lo^{ps} will not think it wisdome in mee, nor to stand with the safety of the present condition of your affaires, to march further with soe inconsiderable a strength as I have. Since I came hither I have made some inquiry into the strength of Abbington, and I heare that it is in such a condition as I much feare it will not be a place for you to rely upon. This towne is of very great consequence, and it is a great prejudice that the fortifications have beene soe neglected. I am much troubled to heare of the enemyes over running most part of Lincolneshire. It cannot but much distract and distress those associated countyes. I heare that the King with his strength was expected at Sherborne on Friday last. If he march speedily into these partes it will concerne your Lo^{ps} to have your forces in as good a posture as you can. My Lords and Gentlemen, I shall alwayes desire to approve my selfe

Your most humble servant,

MANCHESTER.

Reading, 29° Sept. 1644.

POSTSCRIPT.—Since I wrote the other part of my letter I have intelligence that Prince Rupert is come to Welles, and that a good party of the Kinge's horse bend their march for Malborough. I sent this day to view the Castle of Dunington, and I am informed that there is little probability of takeing it without more tyme then it is probable they will have. There are very good gunns, which if they be not tymely brought off they may be in danger to be lost. Your Lo^{ps} will finde that if the King march into these partes Abbington will not be able to resist him, but those men will be a prey unto him. I thought it my duty to give your Lo^{ps} this account, and I referre the determining what shall be done unto your Lo^{ps} wisedomes.

No. 37.—FOR THE COMMITTEE OF BOTH KINGDOMES, &c.

MY LORDS AND GENTLEMEN,

I have received your Lo^{ps} lettre of the 28th of this instant, by which I perceive your Lo^{ps} have given order for the recalling of Colonel Fleetwoode's regiment of horse, which I had appointed to goe into Lincolnshire to their assistance. The number I appointed was by your Lo^{ps} comand, and therefore I hope I have not erred in it. I shall be very glad if those parties may be in such a condicion as they may not want such a strength to releive them. I am misinformed if the enemy within these few dayes be not broken into Lindsey Coste, and plundered and spoyled the country of Lindsey, soe farre as Louthe, soe as most of the people of those partes are fled into Boston for their safety. According to your Lo^{ps} former orders I have left about Oxford Lieutenant-Generall Cromwelles regiment of horse and three troopes of dragoones, with the rest of the horse and foote I am marched thus farre westward. Most of my horse are quartered betwixt Newberry and Basing. I did in my last lettre to your Lo^{ps} take the bouldnesse to acquaint you how unsafe I thought it for me to march further then this place with soe small a number of foote as I yet have with me. When any further strength shall be gathered together in these parts I shall be very ready to doe the best service I can. Your Lo^{ps} very well know the obligacion I haue to those countyes who haue, as farre as in them lay, put this trust upon mee. I receive from them dayly lettres expressing their great trouble that their forces are drawne soe farre from them; and your Lo^{ps} well know that by Ordinance of Parliament these forces are not to be comanded any whether but with the consent of the Comittees of the Associacion. The Comittee for Suffolke sent mee some reasons why they did conceive the distance of these forces might be of sad consequence to them, the which I send your Lo^{ps} here inclosed; it being a duty which I owe both to your Lo^{ps} and to them to represent things cleerly and plainly unto you, and to desire that your comands may be such as that in giveing obedience to your Lo^{ps} I may discharge my duty towards them who have placed this trust in me for their owne security.

My Lords and Gentlemen, I am
Your Lo^{ps} most humble servant,
MANCHESTER.

Reading, 30° Sept. 1644.

No. 38.—TO THE EARLE OF MANCHESTER.

MY LORD,
Sending this bearer, Mr. Cullemburg, Cheife Engineere, to view the towne of Reading and to give his judgment concerning

Mr. Cullenburgh to view Reading.

the fortificacion thereof, wee doe recommend him to your favour, desiring your Lo^p to speake in his behalfe with the Committee there, that when hee shall give his opinion therein meanes may bee providing for the perfecting thereof, and himselfe favoured for his safe journey from thence to Abbington.

Derby House, 30° Septemb^r, 1644.

No. 39.—To the Earle of Manchester.

My Lord,

Your Lo^{ps} lettre of the 30th of September from Reading wee have received, and touching the orders of this Committee for recalling of Colonell Fleetwood's regiment of horse, they were conditionall upon information from Lieutenant-Generall Cromwell that Sir Thomas Glemham with 21 colours of horse was marched from Newarke by Ashby to joyne with other forces, which if it should have proved true Colonell Fleetwood was to returne, and not otherwise. Wee have upon receipt of your Lo^{ps} lettre written to Colonell Fleetwood, if that former information doe not prove true and the enemie bee still in Lincolneshire, to proceed in his journey to Lincolneshire, and there to use his best endeavours against the enemie and for the secureing of those parts. Wee have likewise thought fitt to renew our former desires to your Lo^{pp} to send your horse and foot according to our former orders. Your Lo^p will receive here inclosed a copie of the Ordnance past both Houses, according to the intent whereof wee are considering of persons and instrucions wherewith your Lo^{pp} shall bee acquainted speedily.

Send your horse and foote according to our former orders.

Derby House, 1° Octobris, 1644.

By his Lo^{ps} owne messenger.

No. 40.—To the Earle of Manchester.

My Lord,

Having taken into consideration how prejudiciall delayes have alwaies proved to the publique service, and how necessary it is that your Lo^p should advance speedily westward, wee have thought fitt againe to renew our desires to your Lo^p to send your horse and foot according to our former orders, which wee hope you will doe with that expedition that wee shall not need to iterate ytt againe to your Lo^{pp}. Wee have sent your Lo^p here inclosed a copie of my Lord Generall's lettre with our answer to the same, and of the information wee have received from Sir William Waller.

[marginal note: Send your horse and foot according to former orders.]

Derby House, 2° Octobris, 1644.

By Mr. Binding.

No. 41.—For the Comittee of both Kingdomes, &c.

My Lords and Gentlemen,

Since my last letter to your Lo^{ps} I have received a lettre from Sir William Waller, by the which he certifies me that the King is marching eastward. I had it likewise from my owne scoutes that he quartered upon Wednesday night five miles on this side Dorchester, and that he marches very fast. It is thought by the most and it is reported at Oxford that he will come by Newberry and Abbington, and soe to Oxford. Others think he will bend his course to Winchester, but it is most probable that he will come this way; and therefore I thinke it may be very necessary to hasten the marching of the Citty foote up hether. I shall be ready to doe the best service I can with those forces I have, and therefore I have sent Lieut.-Generall Cromwell to make what hast he can unto me with those horse and dragoones that are with him. This gentleman,

Colonell Sparrow, coming this day to me and acquainting me with the condition of Abbington, I thought it my duty to desire him to wayte upon your Lo^ps and to make a true relacion to you of it, considering I had intelligence of the Kinges march this way. Your Lo^ps may be pleased to thinke of sending downe match and powder for your forces in these partes, for I have lessened my store I brought with me by furnishing of them, and I shall not have enough to serve them and my selfe. I shall dilligently inquire after the King's motions and give your Lo^ps an accompt of them.

My Lords and Gentlemen, I am
    Your Lo^ps most humble servant,
      MANCHESTER.

Reading, 3º Octobr. 1644.

I desire to know your Lo^ps pleasure whether you will have my horse goe to Malborough.

No. 42.—FOR THE COMITTEE OF BOTH KINGDOMES, &c.

MY LORDS AND GENTLEMEN,

I have received your Lo^ps lettres, by which I perceive your Lo^ps remaine unsatisfied with mee for my not marching further westward. In a lettre lately to your Lo^ps I did humbly represent my condicion to you. I have since that time received other lettres from the county of Norfolke by which they represent unto me their feares with their desires that their forces may not be carryed soe farre from them as they heard they were intended; and they did request me to improve my interest in effecting their desires, otherwise they feared they should be disabled as to further recruites or payments of mony. I should faile in my duty both to them and your Lo^ps if I should not declare this unto you. As to my marching further westward, which I conceive is to Newberry, because I had intimacion in a letter that that place was appointed for a rendezvous for my Lord Generalles foote and mine. I have ordered two regiments of foote to lye in Newberry, which is more then the towne can well hold with those forces that are there already of Major-Generall Browne's. The rest of my foot are quartered in this towne and the villages hereabouts, and they shall be within a dayes march of the rendezvous. I confesse I have ordered it in this manner because it gives some satisfaction to the countyes who intrust mee and it refreshes the foote, for whom I have not as yet mony nor clothes, which I expect within few dayes. As for those horse your Lo^{ps} appoint me to send to Malborough, they are thus disposed at this present: Fower troopes I have sent to Baseing at the earnest request of the Comittee of that county; nine troopes lye quartered as near Newberry as they well can, that they may be assistant either to Newberry or Abbington if there be occasion. The rest of those that are with mee lye quartered about this towne. There are twenty troopes of horse and dragoones with Lieut.-Generall Cromwell about Banbury according to your Lo^{ps} comand. Since I came into these partes I have in what way I could beene serviceable to those guarrisones. I received this day a lettre from Major-Generall Browne, which, according to his desire, I thinke fitt to send unto your Lo^{ps}. My Lords and Gentlemen, I hope the publique shall not suffer by my delayes, for I hope it shall appear that I shall not be the last at the rendezvous your Lo^{ps} have appointed. I intend (God willing) to goe myselfe to morrow to Newberry, but shall be here againe by Saturday.

   My Lords and Gentlemen, I am
     Your Lo^{ps} most humble servant,
       [MANCHESTER.]

Reading, 3º Octobris, 1644.

NO. 43.—TO THE EARLE OF MANCHESTER.

MY LORD,
 Wee are advertised from Major-Generall Browne that hee, by a lettre from the Comittee of Essex, understands that Colonell

Sparrowes regiment is to recreut your L^p and to bee putt under new officers. In regard of the consequence of the keeping the towne of Abbington, where that regiment is employed, wee have written to the Committee of Essex that they will take some other course for your Lo^ps recreuts, and that the same regiment may not for the present bee broken, but left as it is for the service of Abbington, from which it cannot bee as yet spared. Wee desire also that you will keepe a constant intelligence with Sir W. Waller and my Lord Generall; and, their horse being now joyned, you will soe order the march of your horse as you may also joyne with them in one body att such place as shall bee most fitt, and to give us speedy notice of what you doe herein. The brigade of the cittie is appointed to march on Monday next; wee desire your Lo^p to appoint two troopes of your horse to bee ready to meet them when they shall bee at Colebrooke. They are, by the order of the House, to bee joyned to your Lo^p or Sir W. Waller, and wee have appointed them to joyne with your Lo^p. Wee have also appointed a troope of horse of Colonell Washborne's to attend that brigade, and desire your Lo^p to appoint the troope of Captayne Middleton to bee another to attend them, unlesse your Lo^p knowes some cause to the contrary, and then wee desire you to appoint some other troope as your Lo^p please for that service.

Derby House, 4° Octobris, 1644.

No. 44.—FOR THE COMITTEE OF BOTH KINGDOMES, &c.

MY LORDS AND GENTLEMEN,

I have received your Lo^ps lettre of the 4th of October. As concerning that regiment under Colonell Sparrow the Comittee for Essex doe much desire that I would take it for part of recreutes for my regiment. But I shall not take upon mee the disposeing of it without your Lo^ps approbation, and shall expect some other course to be taken for my recreutes. I doe observe your Lo^ps comands in keeping constant correspondence with my Lord Generall and Sir William Waller. Most of my horse are quartered in Hungerford and thereaboutes. And I have written to Sir William Waller to let him know that upon any occasion, if he will appoint whether they shall come to him, they shall be ready to serve him. I have appointed two troopes to be ready to wayte upon the citty brigade when they shall be at Colebrooke. As for Captaine Middleton's troope I left it at Huntington to be recreuted, and he is now there. And I beleive those parts at this tyme are in soe great feares as if I shall call him from thence it may prove inconvenient, but if your Lo^{ps} please to comand mee I shall doe it, being always ready to observe your Lo^{ps} comands as

Your Lo^{ps} most humble servant,

MANCHESTER.

Reading, 5° Octob. 1644.

No. 45.—TO THE EARLE OF MANCHESTER.

MY LORD,

Upon consideracion of the information wee have received from Sir William Waller, whereof this enclosed is an extract, wee have thought fitt to desire your Lo^{ps} without any further delay to send all your horse to joyne with my Lord Generall and Sir William Waller's, leaving onely 500 about Banbury and 500 to guard your foot, concerning which wee have likewise written to Lieut.-Generall Cromwell, whereof wee desire your Lo^{pp} to have extraordinary care that it may bee put speedily in execution, and to give us from tyme to tyme notice of your proceedings. Upon advertisement of the surprizall of Crowland wee have written to the Comittee of Cambridge to send 300 foot to Horsey bridge to keepe that passe, or to such place as Lieut.-Governor Treton or Colonel Walton shall appoint. And if any recreuts intended for your Lo^p may bee in readinesse to send them to the Isle of Ely, and to call in the countrey thither and to the towne of Cambridge. Wee have

Send all your horse to joyne with Lord Generalls's without any further delay.

Cambridge to send 300 foote.

Recreuts, if any ready, to bee sent to the Isle of Ely.

40   CROMWELL AND THE EARL OF MANCHESTER.

Nottingham and Derbyshire written too to joyne and attend the enemie.

likewise written to the Yorkshire, Nottingham, and Darbyshire forces, which are joyned in Lincolnshire with your Lo^{ps} forces, to attend the enemies forces in those parts. Upon receipt of your Lo^{ps} lettre of the [5th] of this instant, wherein your Lo^p doth informe us that Captaine Middleton's troope is att Huntingdon, wee desire

Leave Captain Middleton's troope att Huntington.

your Lo^{pp} to leave that troope to bee disposed of by the Comittee of Cambridge for opposeing the enemie that is now fallen into their association. These two troopes which your Lo^p hath appointed to attend the Citty brigade wee desire that they may bee sent to Colebrooke against the morrow att night to convey the [train of artillery] to Reading, to bee sent to my Lord Generall's army, which wee desire your Lo^p to keepe safely till your Lo^p shall understand from my Lord Generall to what place to send the same.

Derby House, 7° Octobris, 1644.

No. 46.—TO THE EARLE OF MANCHESTER.

MY LORDS,

Send your horse upp to Sir W. Waller speedily.

According to our former orders we desire your Lo^p, if your horse bee not already marched, to send them speedily upp to Sir William Waller. Your Lo^p will receive here inclosed the Order of the

Order of the House to march west with all your forces.

House of Commons for your Lo^{ps} marching forthwith westward with your forces, which we desire you accordingly to pursue with all expedition; for the more safe conveighing of my Lord Generall's

Two troopes att Colebrooke to come to Brainford to convey Lord Generall's traine.

trayne of artillery and other carriages we have appointed those two troopes sent by your Lo^p to Colebrooke to come to Brainford, from whence they are to convey the same to your Lo^p. And wee desire your Lo^p to send other two troopes to Colebrooke on Thursday

Send two other troopes to Colebrooke for the cittie brigade.

night to attend the Cittie Brigade.

Derby House, 8° Octobris, 1644.

By HANBURY, sen.

No. 47.—FOR THE COMMITTEE OF BOTH KINGDOMES, &c.

MY LORDS AND GENTLEMEN,

I have received your Lo^{ps} letter, together with an order of the House of Commons, by which I am directed to march westward. I have often received orders from the House of Commons for my marching westward, but they never designed any place to which I should march. I have received comands from your Lo^{ps} formerly to march with my foote to Newberry, which was the place your Lo^{ps} did designe for a rendezvous of my Lord Generall's foote, the Citty forces, and these forces of the associated countyes. According your Lo^{ps} comands my foote have beene, and are still ready at any time within a few howers to be at the rendezvous. If it be your Lo^{ps} intention that I should march further then the place you first appointed, if you please to assigne the place whither you will have me to march I shall obey your comands. I have according to your Lo^{ps} comands ordered two more troopes to march to morrow night to Colebrooke. I did yesterday send orders to those horse that lay at Hungerford to march to Salisbury, and that they should give notice to Sir W. Waller of their readiness to obey his comands.

My Lords and Gentlemen, I am,
    Your Lo^{ps} humble Servant,
        MANCHESTER.

Reading, 9° Octob. 1644.

Since I writt this letter I received intelligence from Sir W. Waller that the King is advancing with his army, and that he intends to retreat according to your Lo^{ps} orders to Marlborough. I only offer this as my humble opinion to you that the sooner your foote come up altogether it will be the more advangeous to your affaires.

No. 48.—To THE EARLE OF MANCHESTER.

MY LORD,

Wee understand by the postscript of your Lo^{ps} letter of the 9th of this instant, that the King's army is marching eastward, upon consideration whereof wee have thought fitt to desire your Lo^{pp} by correspondence with my Lord Generall to agree betweene yourselves upon a convenient place where your foote may meet together soe as they may best keepe the King's army westward. Wee shall use our best endeavours to hasten the citty forces to follow you speedily. Your Lo^p will receive here inclosed the vote this day past the House of Commons.

King marching eastward.

Agree upon a convenient place where your foot may meet together to keepe the King west.

Derby House, 10° Octobris, 1644.

By Craven.

No. 49.—To THE EARLE OF MANCHESTER.

MY LORD,

Having received certaine of the King's advance with all his forces, wee thinke it fitt to send what forces wee can to oppose his march. And therefore desire you immediately to give order to the horse of the regiment of Lieutenant Generall Cromwell that are left behind att or about Banbury, or any of your Lo^{ps} horse that are there, that they forthwith with all expedition march up to the rest of your horse to goe along with the rest of the horse in this service according to former directions. Wee desire your Lo^p according to our former orders by correspondence with my Lord Generall to agree upon a convenient place where your forces may meet together, soe as they may best keepe the King's forces westward, and will bee most for the advantage of the publique service, and soe to looke to the enemies motions as you may not bee hindered to joyne with my Lord Generall for that end.

King advanceth east.

Order Lieut.-Generall Cromwell's horse left about Banbury to march to him.

Agree with Lieut.-Generall for a place to joyne your forces.

Derby House, 11° Octobris, 1644.

By Mr. Potter.

No. 50.—For the Comittee of both Kingdomes, &c.

My Lords and Gentlemen,
I have received your Lo^{ps} letter of the 10th of this instant, and shall accordingly send unto my Lord Generall to know where he will comand me to wayte upon him with those foote I have here. I have likewise received a vote of the House of Commons which orders me to observe such orders as I shall from tyme to tyme receive from your Lo^{ps}, which I am ready to obey. I sent my horse, according to your Lo^{ps} comands, towards Salisbury, but upon the receipt of a letter from Sir W. Waller, by which he gave mee notice he was marched from Shaftesbury towards Marleborough, I called backe my horse to their former quarters, which were neare unto Marlborough. This day I heard from Sir W. Waller, and he desires me to send my horse to Woodford. which accordingly I shall doe. I heare the King with his army is about Blandford.
My Lords and Gentlemen, I am,
Your Lo^{ps} most humble servant,
MANCHESTER.
Reading, 11° Octob. 1644.

I heare that my Lord Generall's traine of artillery will be heare this night. I shall immediatly give my Lord Generall notice of it.

No. 51.—For the Committee of both Kingdomes, &c.

My Lords and Gentlemen,
I have received your letter of the 11th of this instant. I can give you this account, that I have kept intelligence with Lieut.-Generall Cromwell, and as I have heard of the King's advance I have sent him advertisemt thereof and wished him to advance hither. And when I have heard of the King's retreating backe or lyeing still I wished him to remaine in his quarters, because I had no positive

orders to remove his horse from thence. Yet, having intelligence on Thursday last that the King was advanced as farre as Blandford, I sent an order to him to march away with all his horse with what convenient speed he could. And, though I have not heard from him since, yet I believe he is upon his march. I have now this day upon the receipt of your Lo^{ps} letter sent him a copie of it, and have renewed my orders to him for his present marching up to the rest of the horse. I have sent unto my Lord Generall to know what place he will appoint me to attend his comands with the forces I have here, and I cannot tell which way to march untill I doe receive notice from my Lord Generall which way he will direct mee to wayte on him. Those souldiers that are here with mee doe thinke that I am in as fitt a posture to joyne with my Lord Generall as I can be. I take all the care I can to have certaine informacion of the King's motions. I thinke fitt to give your Lo^{ps} notice that my Lord Generall's traine of artillery, money, and carriages came hither the last night.

My Lords and Gentlemen, I am,
Your humble servant,
MANCHESTER.

Reading, 12° Octob. 1644.

Post.—If your Lo^{ps} thinks fitt that I should march to Basing or that way to meet my Lord Generall I shall observe your Lo^{ps} comands. I shall desire to know what your Lo^{ps} will have me doe with the money and traine of artillery.

No. 52.—FOR THE COMMITTEE OF BOTH KINGDOMES, &c.

MY LORDS AND GENTLEMEN,

Since I writt my last letter to your Lo^{ps} I received a letter from my Lord Generall by which he is pleased to let me know that he will not be ready to begin his march till Wednesday. Hee hath likewise sent mee the places of his march from day to day. I intend (God willing) to be about Basingstoake upon Wednesday and soe to have our foote to lye betwixt Newberry and Basingstoake, and there to meet with my Lord Generall. Lieut.-Generall Cromwell is come hither this night. His troopes are yet at Henly, but I have given order they shall march forwards to-morrow, according to your Lo^{ps} direction. I heard this day from Sir W. Waller, who remaines still in the same quarters he was in, and the King remaines still at Blandford, and these quarters he formerly was in. I hear likewise that P. Rupert is bringing the remainder of his forces from Bristoll to the King.

My Lords and Gentlemen, I am,
Your humble servant,

Reading, 14° Octobr. 1644.   MANCHESTER.

No. 53.—TO THE EARLE OF MANCHESTER.

MY LORD,

Your Lo^{ps} of the 12th instant wee have received, whereby we perceive you have written to my Lord Generall for a place of rendezvous. Wee desire you, according to our former orders, that you will in the meane tyme be marching westward the more to hinder the King's advance this way and the sooner to meete the Lord Generall, and for the particular place wee leave that to your Lo^p upon your corresponding with my Lord Generall.

To march westward to hinder the King's advance.

Derby House, 14° Octobris, 1644.

By Mr. Newman.

No. 54.—FOR THE RIGHT HONOURABLE THE COMITTEE OF BOTH KINGDOMES, &c.

MY LORDS AND GENTLEMEN,

I received your Lo^{ps} letter yesterday in the afternoone of the 12th of this instant and shall humbly offer your Lo^{ps} this account that upon the receipt of your Lo^{ps} first letter I sent to his Excellency to know where he would appoint me to wayte on him with these forces under my comaund. But I have not received any answere from my Lord as yet. Upon the comeing hither of my Lord Generall's traine of artillery and mony, I sent againe unto him to let him know of their being here, neither have I received an answere of these letters as yet; therefore, fearcing my former messengers might be intercepted, Mr. Gerrard, who brought the mony, and the Comptroller of the Artillery are gone to Portsmouth to my Lord, and I have againe written to my Lord to certifie him that wheresoever he please to appoint his rendezvous I shall not faile (God willing) to wayte upon him. As for the forces under my command the most of the horse that were with mee are with Sir W. Waller, according to your Lo^{ps} comands. The most of the foote are advanced forward excepting three regimentes that are here for the guard of my Lord Generall's artillery, my owne, and the carriages. Nor can I tell which way to order my march untill I know where my Lord Generall please to appoint me to joyne with him. If the King march this way before wee be conjoyned or before the citty forces come up, I shall desire to know your Lo^{ps} directions whether you will have me engage with those foote and horse I have, joyning my selfe with Sir W. Waller's horse, if I can. If you please to give me a possitive command in this particular I shall punctually observe it, for I hope it shall never be justly sayd that I either decline action or retard it. I shall be glad to serve any of your Lo^{ps} number when they doe come downe.

My Lords and Gentlemen,
Your humble servant,

Reading, 14° Octob. 1644.   MANCHESTER.

My Lords and Gentlemen, I am desired to offer this unto your Lo^{ps} that in regard of our great want of money, whether your Lo^{ps} would be pleased that wee might make use of two thousand pound of this money of my Lord Generall's, and it shall be payd here againe within one weeke. Or if your Lo^{ps} please to furnish us with soe much from London it shall be repayd againe there by Mr. Leman, the treasurer of the association, within a weeke.

No. 55.—To my Lord Generall and Lord Manchester.

My Lords,

The House of Comons hath recomended to this Comittee that some of your Lo^ps forces should be sent to the seige of Bassing for the reduceing of that garrison, which is a service of very great concernment.

Wee desire your Lo^ps being upon the place, and knowing best the state of your forces, to send such of your forces thither for that purpose as you thinke fitt, soe as it may stand with our other affaires which wee have formerly written to your Lo^ps about.

More forces to be sent to Basing.

Darby House, 16° Octobris. 1644.

By Mr. Boyce, Lord Generall Messenger.

No. 56.—For the Committee of both Kingdomes, &c.

My Lords and Gentlemen,

According to advice with Sir W. Waller, and in order to a conjunction with my Lord Generall, I am marched to Basingstoke, and came hither upon Thursday. Yesternight late, I received a very hott allarme from Sir William Waller's quarters that the King with all his army was come to Andover, and that he was upon his retreate towards mee, whereupon I drew out my foote and those horse that were with mee, in order to have done the best service I could for Sir W. Waller's security. But, blessed be God, he is safely retreated hither with little or noe losse. And Sir William Balfour is likewise come hether with my Lord Generall's horse. Upon this alarme I sent to my Lord Generall to advertise him of it, and to desire his speedy advance, who, notwithstanding some difficulties, is marched this night to Alton. Upon this suddaine occasion I tooke upon me to write to Sir James Harrington, to desire him to bring up 4 of the Citty Regiments hither to mee.

I thought it necessary for the safety of Reading to leave one regiment there. If I have erred in this I humbly ask your pardon. I doe not heare that King doth march this day, onely I heare that some of his horse were drawn up about White Church.

My Lords and Gentlemen, I shall be glad to receive your comands, as

Your Lo^{ps} most humble Servant,

MANCHESTER.

Basingstonke, 19° Octobris, 1644.

My Lords and Gentlemen, Wee are both now come hither and can give your Lo^{ps} noe further intelligence then what is conteyned in this letter. Wee are glad to heare that the Citty Regiments are come so neare, and doubt not but you will give my Lord Manchester thankes for that; he desires your pardon. Wee remayne your most humble servants

W. JHONSTON. JO. CREWE.

No. 57.—FOR THE RIGHT HONOURABLE THE COMITTEE OF BOTH KINGDOMES, &c.

MY LORDS AND GENTLEMEN,

Yesterday upon Buckleberry Heath wee received your letter, which gave us hope that the army will shortly receive the provisions which you have sent. The newes of Newcastle came very seasonably unto us, which much encouraged the souldiers, and soe affected them that many of the regiments went presently of their own accord to solemne prayer. The army, about an hower before night, came within a myle and within view of the enemy, who was drawne forth in a body upon a place of advantage neere Newberry. Our dragoones and theirs fired one upon another for two howers; twenty of our horses were killed, but not one of our men lost. A Captaine of our horse, who came up in the vann, was shott in the thigh, six of the clock in the evening. It was resolved last night that the field should be viewed by the chiefe officers early this morning. It will be an advantage to us to set upon his army on this side Newberry, because wee shall be betwixt the enemy and our provisions; and to fall upon him on the other side, because we shall be betwixt the enemy and Prince Rupert, who is dayly expected with additional forces; the ground not having beene viewed they could determine nothing herein. Being informed by those that came from London that they met many souldiers going homewards, wee renew our desire that some exemplary punishment may be inflicted upon them. Wee remaine,

    My Lorde,
      Your Lo^{ps} humble servants,
        W. JHONSTON, JO. CREWE.
Thatcham, 26° Octob. 1644.

Wee have had a faire night (blessed be God), and hope for a faire day.

No. 58.—FOR THE RIGHT HONOURABLE THE COMITTEE OF BOTH KINGDOMES, &c.

MY LORDS AND GENTLEMEN,

The forces mentioned in our last lettre came from Wickam Heath towards the place where the King's forces were drawn up, betweene Dennington and Newberry, neere the Castle, having noe way to passe but by a wood and through laynes. Wee mett workes and fortifications crossing those laynes which they had at night beene casting up, and wherein they planted ordinance; they had also other ordinance, two bodyes of their horse and two brigades of foote, at a little distance. They played also from the Castle upon our men with great shott; they were hard to gayne, yet it pleased God soe to incourage the [their?] spirit, among whom my Lord Generall's forces had a most speciall care, and soe to blesse their endeavors, that about five a clocke (which was but the space of an hower after their falling to worke) they tooke it by storming, and got 4 peece of ordnance; afterwards, beating the enemy of his ground, they got other five ordnance; my Lord Generall's foote tooke much contentment in regaining some of their ordnance. Our horse stood very gallantly under the view and danger of the canon playing directly upon them when they were drawing themselves together to secure the foote, and in charging the enemy put them to a retreate, and hath taken the Earle of Cleveland, who had that brigade.

That all the generall officers did very resolutely their partes; my Lord of Manchester fell upon the other passe in a seasonable tyme.

Your Lo^{rs} most humble servants,

W. JHONSTON, JO. CREWE.

From our league betweene Dennington and Newberry,
27° Octobris, 1644.

No. 59.—FOR THE RIGHT HONOURABLE THE COMMITTEE OF BOTH KINGDOMES, &c.

MY LORDS AND GENTLEMEN,

As wee wrote in our last lettre, and as we repeate lest that should miscarry, yesterday, about 4 of the clocke, those forces which went from Thatcham towards Newberry by the way of Wickam Heath and were there drawen up set upon a worke and breast-worke, well guarded with ordnance, horse, and foote, which commanded all the wayes which lead to that side of the field betwixt Newberry and Dennington Castle, where the King's army was drawne up. The workes were made strong, although they had but little tyme, that the gaineing of them would have lost much tyme and beene doubtfull if the foote (amongst whom my Lord Generalles particular forces deserved very well) had not with extraordinary resolution stormed them, which they did within an hower after the first charge. Upon their unexpected entrance into the workes their foote which secured them all ran and left the ordnance that were placed in and about the workes. Maior Generall Skippon hazarded himselfe to much. Sir W. Balfour used great dilligence, there being but few field officers of horse. Sir William Waller, Sir Arth. Hesilrige, Sir James Harrington, Lieut.-Generall Middleton, Lieut.-Generall Cromwell, Major-Generall Crawford, Major-Generall Holborne, Coll. Greemes, and diverse others did very good service. The Earle of Manchester, about 4 of the clocke, endeavoured to force a passage through Shaw, a village on the other side of the field where the King's forces lay. P. Maurice was on that side, and many of the King's best foote, who maintained those passes, although they were very bravely assaulted. The Earle of Manchester for want of day light and by reason of the great guards did not take the passages; but his employing soe many of the King's forces on that side was of great advantage to our other forces. The battaile lasted about three howers. They fought at least an hower by mooneshine. The Earle of Manchester and those on the other side were ignorant of each others successe till the next morning. The Earle of Cleveland was taken prisoner and is sent up to London, and, as wee heare, Colonell Goring's younger brother was slayne. Captaine Galler, one of my Lord Generall's captaines, was slaine. Our side tooke nine pieces of ordnance. Major Skippon guesseth that the number slaine on both sides were betweene two and three hundred. The King's forces were all gone before this morning. Some few carts were left on the field, but the carriages were put into Dennington Castle and soe neare it that they could not be taken off. All our horse and dragoones, except 1000 which stay with the Earle of Manchester, are gone after the King's forces, which wee heare are gone toward Wallingford. Wee desire you to take into your consideracon how the foote army shall be disposed, and how they may be provided for; none of your provisions are as yet come, but wee hope will be shortly. Wee desire to give God the glory of this victory, it being His worke and upon His day. The Earle of Manchester marcheth to-morrow to Blewbury. We rest, my Lords,

Your Lo^{ps} humble servants,

W. JHONSTON. JO. CREWE.

Newbury, 28° Octob. 1844.

Wee earnestly entreat you to take care that the want of chirurgeons may be supplyed. It is a miserable thing to see men want meanes of cure who have beene wounded in the defence of the publique.

No. 60.—To my Lord Manchester and the Comanders-in-Chiefe.

My Lords and Gentlemen,

Understanding by my Lord Wareston and Mr. Crew that it was the unanimous opinion of a Councell of Warre that the carriages necessary for the army cannot passe to Abbington, and that the forces should continue united at Newbury and thereabouts till the King's army went to winter quarters, wee stayed a lettre written from the Houses for your advancing forward till this morning, to the end wee might acquaint them in generall that the opinion of a Councell of Warre upon the place was for another way. Upon which report from this Comittee the Houses have appointed that their lettre should not be sent. Wee have given you notice hereof with all speed, and leave it to you, if you thinke fitt, to goe backe with your foote to Newbury, and to make the best use you can of your horses and dragoones. Wee desire you to keepe your forces together, and to endeavour to take in Denington Castle. Battering peeces and amunicion will be quickly with you for that purpose. Wee recommend unto you the sending a regiment to Basing, and to have an eye to all the notions of the enemy in the meane tyme.

Opinion of Councell of Warre to stay the army about Newbury.

Houses' lettre not to goe.

Left to them upon the place.

To take Denington Castle.

A regiment to Basing.

Darby House, 5° November, 1644.

By Durant, at 12 morn.

No. 61.—For the Right Honourable the Committee of
both Kingdomes.

My Lords and Gentlemen,
I have reccieved your Lo^{ps} lettre of the 5th of this instant, and acquainted the rest of the Comanders-in-Chiefe with the contents of your Lo^{ps} lettre, and accordingly wee are all this night come to Newbury. Wee have very uncertaine intelligence where the enemy is, but wee heare his intentions are to fetch the artillery and amunicion in Denington Castle. I thought fitt to give your Lo^{ps} what we heare of the enemyes motions, and what is done by us.
    My Lords and Gentlemen, I am,
      Your Lo^{ps} humble servant,
        Manchester.
Newbury, 6° November, 1644.

No. 62.—To my Lord Manchester and the Comanders-in-Cheife.

My Lord and Gentlemen,
By the inclosed Order you see the minde of the House concerning Basing and Wiltshire, which wee recommend to your speciall care and speedy execution. Wee are of opinion that the Citty Regiment which hath beene all this tyme in Reading may most fitly be sent to Basing, and in the roome thereof a regiment of my Lord Manchester's, or such other as you thinke fitt may be put into Reading. The regiment being sent to Basing wee desire that Colonell Ludlow's Regiment of horse may be sent into Wiltshire, and this to be done with all expedition.

Concerning Basing and Wiltshire. The Citty regiment at Reading to be sent to Basing.

Darby House, 6° November, 1664.
 By Bulmer.

No. 63.—To my Lord Manchester.

My Lord,

By the copie enclosed your Lo^p sees what intelligence wee have received. Wee desire by all meanes you can to enforme yourselves of the certainty thereof, and if you finde the intelligence to be true, to send after them such a body of horse as may prevent them either in spoyling and plundering the country, or attempting any guarrisons, or maching toward the associacion, which wee recomend to your especiall care.

To send after the enemy a body of horse.

Darby House, 6° Novembris, 1644.

By Bulmer.

No. 64.—For the Committee of both Kingdomes, &c.

My Lords and Gentlemen,

I received two lettres from your Lo^{ps} the last night, both of them of the 26th of this instant, and they have beene comunicated to the rest of the comanders-in-chiefe. All our intelligence is that the King is come to Wallingford with his whole army, and that he intends to march to Dennington Castle. And therefore, their opinion is, that it is not safe to make any division of our forces untill we know certainely what the intentions of the enemy are. I hope a day or two will discover what wee shall resolve of, which I shall acquaint your Lo^{ps}. I have nothing else at present to offer to you but the service of

Your Lo^{ps} humble servant,

MANCHESTER.

Newberry, 8° Novemb. 1644.

No. 65.—For the Committee of both Kingdomes, &c.

My Lords and Gentlemen,

Yesterday, late in the evening, wee had certaine intelligence that the enemies' whole army were within 5 or 6 mile of us. And this day, betwixt 10 and 11 of the clocke, they drew up to Dennington Castle, and from thence, they both with their horse and foote drew into a plaine field betweene the towne Newberry and the Castle. It was not held safe for us to draw out, in regard the Castle by their ordnance would have done much spoyle upon us. Therefore wee resolved to make good the towne. The enemy came on upon us, but by the blessing of God he received such a repulse as that he is retreated. And the night falling on wee could not pursue them. But wee have sent out scouts to observe their motions, and doe intend to follow them. Wee shall have a particular care of the towne of Reading, according to your Lo^{ps} comands in your lettre of the 8th of November, which wee received this night.

My Lords and Gentlemen, wee have nothing more to give your Lo^{ps} an account of, but rest

Your Lo^{ps} humble servantes,
MANCHESTER.
WILLIAM WALLER.
W. BALFOUR.

Newberry, 9° Novemb. 1644.

No. 66.—For the Committee of both Kingdomes, &c.

My Lords and Gentlemen,

By our last wee gave your Lo^{ps} an account of the King's attempts to force us out of Newberry. It was impossible for us to hinder the King from takeing his traine out of the Castle, and to keepe the towne of Newberry, he comeing with soe considerable an army, for had wee drawne up between the Castle and the King, the King had wheeled about and possessed the towne. Then the weather and want would have driven us to a retreate. The King would not only have his traine, but the towne as a quarter, and Basing releived, and that had been the best. Wee heare the last night he drew out some of his traine, and sent it to Wallingford. This morning early wee found him drawne up in battalia, both horse and foote, about a mile from the Castle. Wee drew out, intending to have falne upon his army. But considering his many advantages of ground and the weather falling bad, following might breake our army, the officers of the foote complaining of the lessening of their foote, and many hundreds of our horses be already dead, and the living very weake, and many of the troopers run from their colours. And being assured that upon our quitting Newberry the enemy would forthwith take it, wee thought it fittest to returne to Newberry, where wee now are watching the King's motions and waiting your Lo^{ps} further orders. And in the meane tyme wee will do what to our best understandings wee apprehend fittest for the publique, and are

Your Lo^{ps} humble servantes,
MANCHESTER.
WILLIAM WALLER.
W. BALFOUR.

Newberry, 10 November, 1644.

No. 67.—TO THE EARLE OF MANCHESTER, COMANDER-IN-CHEIFE IN THE ARMY.

MY LORD AND GENTLEMEN,

This morning wee received your lettre of the 8th of this instant, by which wee understand that the King is come to Wallingford with his whole army, and that hee intends to march to Dennington Castle, and wee are very glad that you have taken that resolution which was our advise to you in our last letter, that it is not safe to divide your forces untill you know certainly what the intentions of the enemie are, concerning whose motions and your resolutions wee desire you to send us frequent intelligence.

Send us frequent intelligence of the enemies motions and your resolutions.

Darby House, 9° November, 1644.

By Durant.

No. 68.—For the Committee of both Kingdomes, &c.

My Lords and Gentlemen,

It is the desire of the chiefe officers in these armyes that your Lo^{ps} may have a right understanding of this late action of the King's advance towards us, and of his releiveing of Dennington Castle, and therefore they have thought it fitter that Sir Arthur Hesilrig, who was present here, should give your Lo^{ps} an account of it, then to make a relation of it by letter. We haveing nothing further to offer to your Lo^{ps} but the service of

Your Lo^{ps} most humble servants,

                Manchester.
                William Waller.
                W. Balfour.

Newberry, 12° November, 1644.

No. 69.—To my Lord Manchester and the rest of the Commanders, &c.

My Lord and Gentlemen,

Wee have received your letters concerning the releife of Dennington Castle by the enemie, and are very sory that they mett not with that opposition that was expected from an army that God had blessed lately with soe happy a victorie against them. Soe long as the enemie continues in the field, wee cannot advise that you should goe to your winter quarters, but are very desirous that,

Sorry the King's army was not opposed.

CROMWELL AND THE EARL OF MANCHESTER.

Keepe your forces together whilst the King is in the field. keeping your forces together, you will use your best endeavours to recover the advantage the enemie hath lately gained in releiving Dennington.

This upon consideracion of the present posture of affaires wee have thought fitt to advise, but leave it you who are upon the place if you find reason to the contrary to doe therein as you shall thinke most for the advantage of the publique. And because the *Prevent the releife of Basing.* enemie probably doth intend the releife of Basing, wee recommend it to your speciall care to prevent that designe, which not prevented would exceedingly encourage the enemie and bee very *Wee cannot send comissioners into the army.* prejudicall to the publique affaires. Diverse of this Committee goe along with the propositions of peace, soe that wee cannot for the present send any to the army. And, that all your affaires may bee managed with the greater unanimitie and executed with the *Your undertakings to bee resolved by common advise.* more cheefulnesse, it is our desire that all your undertakings and enterprises bee resolved upon by common advise of a councell of warre, and from time to time give us frequent advertisements of your proceedings.

Darby House, 12° Novemb. 1644.

By Mr. Hanbury.

NARRATIVE

OF THE

EARL OF MANCHESTER'S CAMPAIGN.

[a] In the beginning at my coming into the Earle of Manchester's army in February last I was commanded to goe with Cromwell towards Hilsdan Howse, which was taken, and so ordered to continue about Buckingam and thereabouts with both horse and foote. Cromwell went to Cambridge for the further settlement of things there, and in his absence one Leiftenant Paker,[b] a notorious Anabaptist, disobeyed Major-General Craufurd's orders neere Bedford, whereupon the head of the armie gave the said Paker a sore cheque and putt him in arest, so that the said Paker complayned to the said Cromwell, who uppon my returne to Cambridge sent Leiftenant Coll. Rich[c] to signifie unto mee that I did exceeding ill in chequing such a man which was not well taken, *hee being a Godly man*,[d] and so further of that there was no more. At Stanford uppon our advance to Lincolne for the reduceing of it there was a party of horse sent out uppon intelligence given of the Earle of Newcastle's horse coming to Tuxford and Mansfeild, and Cromwell went with it towards Lincolne [e] but did nothing at all; and shortly after wee

[a] This appears to be the document mentioned by Carlyle.—*Cromwell's Letters*, &c. vol. i. p. 242.—G.C.
[b] Packer. This is not John Packer the proprietor of Donnington Castle but Robert Packer, afterwards a Major-General.—G.C.
[c] One of the most trusted officers of Horse. Colonel Rich, however, attempted to betray Cromwell during the Protectorate.—G.C.
[d] Underscored by a subsequent hand.
[e] " towards Lincolne " added by another hand.

advanced to Lincolne, which was taken, and so shortly after that my Lord of Manchester did joyne his forses with the Scots and my Lord Fairfax in the takeing in of Yorke in the aforesaid tyme from the beginning of our coming out from Cambridge till wee came to Lincolne. The sinister endes of Cromwell weare not knowne but by the putting out of all brave gentlemen in the army by false suggestions to my Lord and bringing in of others in theire places, whoe afterward proved traytors and cowards, and still fomenting further mischeife in the army, notably seconded by Pickering. Before Yorke, our horse being absent from my Lord of Manchester in pretence of doeing good service to the publicque, Cromwell and his creatures did nothing but foment sedition and dissention in my Lord's army of horse, in so much that hee, to withdrawe the hearts of people from the Earle of Manchester, by some sinister and pernitious course hee framed a petition which was managed by Leiftenant-Collonell Whaley and Leiftenant-Coll. Lilburne, and in the procurcing of the officers' hands unto it, sundry denying the underwriting thereof, as Cap. John and Samuell Moody, Cap. Pattison, Cap. Arminger, Cap. La Hunte, and Major Wilde, who uppon there refusall weare threatened with these words: "Take heede what they did, for it was to goe through the army, *and Cromwell did take an accounte who had not underwrytten it, mutche wilifieing them that did not*.ᵃ The petition was of such stuff that it was highly mutinous, and to putt out all men out of the armie that were not Brownists, or of such like sects, much diminishing my Lord's honor and the rest of the gentlemen in the army. The Petition is still extant in Cromwell's hands; so that uppon the takeing of Yorke articles weare granted to the enemy to march away with armes and baggage, who weare upon the way, notwithstanding the safe conduct from the three generalls, robbed, and most what they had taken from them by my Lord of Manchester's horse, of whom a Leiftenant and many troopers and other officers weare taken and brought before a Martialls Court at Doncaster, where Cromwell thrust

ᵃ The words underscored are interlined by another hand.

himselfe without order, or law, to bee president. It was found in the court that the Leiftenant was highly guilty of the robbery with all the rest. Notwithstanding all that hee, haveing the *name of a Godly man, beeing an Independant*, was sett at liberty by Cromwell, which highly incensed our enemies for our falshood against them at Doncaster. Major-General Craufurd was sent into Darbyshire with a party of my Lord of Manchester's army for the reduceing of that country to the obedience of the Parliament, which after it was done by command the said Craufurd returned with the army to Lincolne. At that tyme there weare severall letters too the Committee of both Kingdomes to my Lord of Manchester for the sending of a strong party into Cheschire, and so resolved so soone as the Major-Generall came home that the party should goe, which was accordingly ordered under the command of Coll. Wermonden, and uppon theire march another order came from the Committee of both Kingdomes commanding my Lord of Manchester to march with his army into the west, which presently was done; and if the highe [a] of mutinie by Cromwell and his juncto who endevoured the hindring of the army by perswading them to a mutiny would have bine sooner and more able to putt things in execution then was done. However, my Lord of Manchester to testifie his willingness did march by 12 or 14 miles a day, no less. At that tyme my Lord of Manchester had enough to doe to keepe the army from mutining, being put on by Cromwell and his juncto, who absolutely refused orders from Major-Generall Craufurd, especially *Coll. Pickering's and Mountagne's regiments.*[b] These heavy distractions invented by Cromwell hee went on in a most high way, and, to shew his power in the army against those who weare the refusers to underwrite the scandalous petition, he outed Cap. Arminger, who was sent, and by leave of his Collonell, to London, and his troope given away to a notorious Independent, who uppon the receiveing of it into his charge the said Cromwell command-

[a] Something seems to have been omitted here.
[b] Underlined to note that they were partizans of Cromwell.—G.C.

ing the said Fleetwood to cashire the whole troope and putt in none but Independents, that theire pernitious endes might the better bee accomplished, which accordingly was done. All this tyme the said Cromwell endevoured to worke Major-Generall Craufurd's ruine by diswading the Earle of Manchester's army not to obey him, and, giveing his charge away to others, makeing them to doe the duty, did in the most notorious manner traduce and callumneate the said Craufurd to make him odious to the army and to discontent him, that so hee the said Cromwell the better might advance his wicked endes, uttering many speeches highly to his disadvantage and utter ruine, and for drawing of factions in the army, which highly distracted the publique good in Lincolne, who still sate at theire consultations how to insult over my Lord of Manchester and his army, and still continuing uppon theire mischeivous actions in fomenting of mischeife all the way betweene Lincolne and Huntington; the said Cromwell attributing [a] *all the praise to himselfe* of other *men's actions, whose only reason was to* cloud those who desiered to doe good servise. The pressing desiers the Earle of Manchester had to putt in execution the Committee of both Kingdomes there commands for the joyneing with my Lord of Essex, and his releife of Abington at his first coming to Reading, was cleerely demonstrated by his willingness in sending necessaries which they stood in neede of at Abington, and wayting uppon Cromwell's returne from Banbury, which action there deserves notice to bee taken of it. Uppon his Excellence's first letter from Portsmouth to the Earle of Manchester for a conjunction, my Lord of Manchester marched away to Baseing with his foote and a fewe troopes of horse, sending all the most parte of the horse to joyne with Sir William Waller at Sallsbury, who weare repulsed [b] and forsed to retire to Basing, my Lord of Manchester's resolution there beeing so bent

[a] By means of the Press. Military reputations were much helped by the Diurnals. It is probable that Cromwell did not reject the overtures of special correspondents as Colonel Hutchinson did. His name is often mentioned.—G.C.

[b] At Andover.—G.C.

for fighting that hee himselfe, my Lord Wareston, Sir William Balfore, Major-Generall Skippon, with diverse others, went to looke uppon the fields, that, if the enemie advanced, to sett out the place every army should stand uppon, which was seconded by his Excellencie the Earle of Essex at his coming to Basing; and for the subsistence of the armies at Basing-Stoke it was concluded to march to Redding and so to come uppon the other side of the Kennet upon the enemy, and to forse the King to fight, notwithstanding the enemy beeing in theire strength, my Lord of Essex beeing in Redding leaft sicke. As it was concluded so it was performed, that in the latter ende of October; the result of the first debate beeing that Major-Generall Craufurd should march about with the Earle of Manchester's foote and all the cavalry, saveing 1,000,[a] which should stay by the foote uppon the hills neere Dolman's howse; and after Major-Generall Craufurd had orders to march the first result was alltered, and the seacond was that Major-Generall Skippon and the citisens should march about to Spen Hill,[b] and Craufurd to stay uppon the hill neere Dollman's howse; so that night the enemy not beeing so much as allarumed, the next day both horse and foote as is mentioned marched where they came about 3 of the clock in the afternoone, where both our armies and the enemy began to play uppon one another with greate canon and about 4 a clock began to play with musquetts. Uppon the right wing was Sir William Balford (*i.e.* Balfour) and upon the leaft wing Lieftenant-Generall Cromwell with my Lord of Manchester's horse, the bodies of foote advanceing engaged with the enemy, that by the report of the best there, if Cromwell had played the parte that became him, the enemie had bine totally routed; all the horse under his command stood still when *Coll. Bartklett*[c] *brigade was charged three tyms.* Notwithstanding all that they *stood still, Cromwell himselfe* not beeing *uppon the head of them*[d] Generall

[a] Under Ludlow.—G.C.   [b] Making a wide circuit of Donnington Castle.—G.C.
[c] *i.e.* Berkeley,—G.C.
[d] See the Earl of Manchester's statement as given by Rushwood.—G. C.

Leiftenant Middleton came seeing so greate absurdities and oversights, and desired the said Cromwell's horse to charge, who refused him till hee went with one of the squadrons and charged the enemy, who was routed and lefte on secconded to fly for his life, beeing in the middle of his enemies, so that day there was no servise performed att all by Cromwell. Night came on, the enemy marched away in the night in great disorder, in so much that the van was at Wallingforde when the reare was at Dunnington. Notwithstanding of Cromwell's knowledge of the enemies running, there was no course taken for the preventing of theire running away, which by Cromwell's horse should have bine performed. Both Major-Generall Skippon, Coll. Barklett, and Coll. Dawies intimateing theire running unto the head of the horse, and nothing done till the next day at nyne a clock in the morneing, where they had not so much as a scout out to know if the enemy weare gone or not, neither was there any sent unto the Earl of Manchester to lett him know of theire goeing till about eight in the morneing.[a] My Lord of Manchester in the day preceding did labour with a greate deale of toyle and greate danger of his life, in so much that the men who weare *ryding*[b] with him weare shott. Notwithstanding these greate dangers hee was in hee endeavoured the utmost of his abilities by rideing to and fro and commanding things to bee putt in execution as first in the morneing. Hee commanded a party of 400 musqueteers to falle over the little river which passes by Dunington Castle, over a bridge, which most dextrously hee commanded the night before, to prepare for the diversion[c] of the King's forces from goeing to Spen Hill, where they learned in the morneing our greatest force was a marching, which accordingly was done, and if

---

[a] This statement seems to show that Cromwell was quite as much in fault as the Earl of Manchester.—G.C.

[b] Inserted in the margin by another hand.

[c] A rather perilous manœuvre on the part of the Earl of Manchester, as it might have drawn the whole of the King's forces upon him—for at this time the rest of the Parliament army were making their flank march.—G.C.

those who weare commanded had not exceeded theire commission [they] would have had greate victory, and as it was they tooke two workes from the enemy, wherein they tooke a captayne and severall prisoners, and advanced too farr without order and weare repulsed, to the greate greife of the Earle of Manchester. So that tyme the Earle of Manchester did continue in his very greate toyling to prepare the falling uppon the enemy in and neere Dollman's howse, and above 500 commanded musqueteeres, commanded for the falling on first as forlorne hope, which to the amazement of the enemy weare severall tymes drawne on and off, and at last they fell on, seconded by the severall brigades of foote. If the forwardness of Major-Generall Craufurd's regiment had been seconded the howse and garden had bine gayned, but they weare bett off with the loss of one of Major-Generall Craufurd's collours and twoe drakes, lost for want of lookeing unto beeing carried headlong on; *the faulte of the losing of the draks was Capiten Hamond.*^a The next morneing a councell of warr was called at Speen, the result whereof was that the horse should followe the pursuite of the enemy, who went no further then to Blewbery and thereabouts, gieving the enemy all the advantages in the world, so that in few dayes following wee marched with the foote to Blewbery and Hagburne, Harwell and Chilton, where wee resolved in a councell of warr to stay till wee received orders from the Committee of both kingdomes; uppon the receipt whereof wee marched the whole army, both horse and foote, and quartered the foote in Newbery and thereabout, and the horse betweene Redding and Hungerford, uppon both sides of the Kennett, where wee continued with a constant resolution to fight the enemy and to prevent the relieveing of Dunnington Castle, and to that purpose Major-Generall Skippon and Major-Generall Craufurd were sent to looke upon the feilds, and

---

^a Words underscored interlined by another hand.

This is probably Colonel Robert Hammond, afterwards the King's gaoler at Carisbrook. The passage seems like a covert insinuation that there was wilful neglect on the part of Hammond.—G.C.

so resolved to meete the enemy *neer*[a] *Dennington Castle towards Compton Downs upon Bussoke*[b] *Heath*, and if our intelligence had bine good we had accordinglie followed our resolutions. The enemy did advance towards Wallingford, of whose motions wee had dayly good intelligence till the very instant of the enemies advance, the length of Compton Dounes. At five o'clock at night a leiftenant of the enemies did come to Newberry to Sir William Balfore's howse, where my L^d of Manchester was, who related that the enemy was in his march uppon Compton Downes with a resolution to fight, and reported to bee 15,000 horse and foote, so that instantly all the commanders-in-chiefes weare called to a councell of war, the result whereof was to drawe very early all the horse into Newberry Wash, which was not performed. The enemy marching very furiously came in view at Dunnington Castle, where not so much as one to oppose them, farr less such numbers as became to knowe of the enemies motions. The enemie presently drew over the little river[c] at Dunnington to Speene Fields, where the enemy posessed themselves, which, without all peradventure, if our horse had bine according to the hower appointed, we had beaten the enemies army *regiment after*[d] regiment as they marched over the narrow passages before they should have come to the posture of fighting. *Major-General Skippon railling uppon the horss on the head of the armie*[d] upon the feilds before Newbery Townes ende, and in a little howse in Newbery Towne, and towards Schew, wee held councells what to doe, the result whereof was that wee could not fight the enemy upon the feild before Newbery, the Castle of Dunnington commanding all that feild with theire ordinance; *al the officers of horss mutche aganst drawing the horss throghe the toune from Newbery wasche*, saying that

[a] Interlined by the other hand.
[b] Bussock is about a mile and a half northward of Donnington Castle. Here are the remains of Roman encampments. It seems to be the place alluded to by Clarendon in his account of the relief of the Castle 9th November, 1644.—G.C.
[c] The Lamborne.—G.C.
[d] Interlined by the other hand.

*the horss could not stand without great danger of the great losse.*ᵃ My L^d of Manchester said what ever was thought fitt by the councell of warr hee should bee *very very*ᵇ well contented, and so acte. But some weare for fighting and drawcing the whole force into the feilds *befor Newburry,* but opposed by others, especially Major-Generall Skippon, Middleton, Craufurd; and Hoburne tolde that if they continued uppon that posture wee resolved uppon wee would suffer dishonor and bee buried quick. The enemy weare about 12,000 horse and foote resolved to fight us, wee in our trenches lookeing uppon them, a body of horse charged our horse, who routed ours and beatt them into our foote, but our foote received the enemy very bravely and repulsed them, so that Major-Generall Craufurd, not one of the officers of the horse in chiefe *excepting Sir William Balfour*ᶜ there, marched towards the enemy and made them give ground, in so much that if our horse had come to us wee had undoubtedly routed the enemy. So the night came on. Then Cromwell and the horse began to come through the towne when all was done, so about 8 o'clock at night wee knew of the enemyes marching away, it was resolved that all the horse should follow the enemy *the nexte morninge by the breake of day.*ᵈ At 9ᵉ o'clock the next morneing all the horse weare standing uppon the feild neere Dollman's howse, so that Major-Generall Craufurd presently drew the Earle of Manchester's foote to the horse at Dollman's howse. So then, all the comanders-in-chiefe rideing to the topp of a hill to looke uppon the enemy, Major-Generall Craufurd desired wee might fall uppon them in the reare before they went away. My Lord of Manchester answered, With all my hart, what wee doe lett it be qu¹ckly done. Sir Arthure Haselrigg and Cromwell enquireing of mee the way of it how I could doe it, I told them that it beeing so neere I desired that 3,000 horse and a musqueteir behinde every one,ᶠ to plant in the hedges,

---

ᵃ Interlined by the other hand. ᵇ *Sic.*
ᶜ Interlined as before. ᵈ The like
ᵉ Originally written "8." ᶠ A common practice in those times.—G.C.

might be sent and the rest to follow,[a] which undoubtedly would be the only way. Cromwell said that the horse was so weake it could not bee, so presently my Lord of Manchester said, Gentlemen, lett us doe quickly what wee doe, so that presently all the commanders-in-cheife wente to a little howse on the head of the army, where Sir Arthure Haselrig[b] entered in speech first, saying that the King did march in a very good posture and that he was stronger than hee expected them to bee, and made a very regulare retreate; that it was impossible for us to come at him without greate disadvantage, and that it was not councellable to fight them or follow them, for our horse was very weake, and though wee beate the King hee would still bee King, and wee should not be able to doe any good uppon any of his garrisons, nor take any of them, for his army was a greate deale more true unto him than ours was, and though they should bee routed they would gather themselves togeather againe, and if the King beat us the kingdome of England would bee lost, for neither officers nor garrisons would make any of our runners stand, but bee a meanes to loose Abington, Redding, and all other places. More, hee would not only be able to overrun all the country where the Parliament friends are, and drawe a greate party to himselfe by such an overthrowe, and would bee able to goe to the very gates of London, and wee had no meanes to shun it or keepe him back, neither was there any reliefe neerer than Newcastle which we might expect, no releife so suddenly from it, and so if wee followed the King, considering the weakeness of our horse and the feweness in number, as hee supposed them not to exceede my Lord Generall's 1,000, Sir William Waller's 1,500, and my Lord of Manchester's 2,000; but to lye still at Nubery with our foote and to quarter our horse as neere as can be to attend the enemies motions, whereby wee might bee able to enterpose betweene them and Basing, and so not to lett them poppe into Nube[rry], and so further bee a meanes to releive Basing and the looseing of Nubery, all which hee humbly

[a] Interlined as before.
[b] Sir Arthur Haselrigg was always a timorous counsellor in the field.— G.C.

conceived was the best; and so Cromwell presently speakeing did in these same very words make a speech very neere a quarter of an hower ; so that all joyning did presently order the foote to Newbery, and the horse thereabouts. Awhile after there came letters to Major-Generall Craufurd, the substance whereof was that all the blame at London lay uppon Manchester, Middleton, Craufurd, and Hoburn; and this letter was seconded by a letter from the Committee, which, though in downe right termes did not say wee weare to blame, but so much that nothing should be done without a joint consent of the whole councell of warr, which letters much touched my Lord of Manchester and the most parte of the commanders-in-cheife ; and in my Lord of Manchester's lodging in Newbery, in the presence of my Lord of Manchester, Sir William Belfore, Sir William Waller, Major-Generall Skippon, Coll. Barklet, and Major-Generall-Craufurd, Cromwell did say, finding my Lord of Manchester much moved at the aforesaid letters after hee reads it twice over, that hee found nothing in the letter but what may bee written without reflexion uppon any, and told my Lord of Manchester: My Lord, I hold him for a villain and a knave that would doe any man ill offices, but there was nothing done but what was justifiable and by the joint consent of the councell of warr, and that there was nothing done but what was answerable. So uppon that councell of warr there was presently thought fitt that there should bee a letter drawne and sent to the Committee of both Kingdomes representing the whole condition of the army, which was referred to bee done by Leif.-Generall Cromwell, which accordingly was done, wherein hee gave a full relation of the weakeness of the army, which, considering the wayes hee has gone, much deserves your notice takeing of it. So allwayes it was held fitt in all councells of warrs, by reason of the greate consequence both Abington and Reading weare unto us, to continue our quarters at Newbery, and so to waite uppon the enemies motions. So that our intelligence was that Prince Rupart had an intention to releive Basing House with a party of horse, which to prevent it was ordered by a councell of warr that the three armies of horse should releive one another for the hindring of that designe, which accordingly was done. So, uppon our intelligence of the King's remove from Marlburrow, it was supposed hee was marching to Basing to releive it with his army, wee conceived it fitting to march that day to Oldermeiston, where wee continued upon the feilds, and if the enemy went to Baseing to endevour to intercept him; and so at Oldermeiston at a councell of warr, where the question was only whether it was councellable to fight or not, and concluded by all, no man speaking so much against fighting as Cromwell, and so unanimously consenting not to fight, but to endeavour to hinder the releife of Baseing, or to withdrawe the forces which weare lying before Baseing, and so to keepe our armies intire, dividing ourselves the foote at Redding and Henly and our horse all about Fernham, Okingham, Windsor, Maydenhead, and Stwins.

[Endorsed] "A brieff recollection of passages in my Lord of Manchester's armie."[a] [" *From*[b] *Maior-Gener.*"[c]

[a] In the same handwriting as the interlineations.
[b] Major-General Cranfurd. It seems likely that the interlineations may be those of Sir William Balfour. This narrative, like that which bears the name of Cromwell, omits all mention of the failure of the combined forces to take Donnington Castle, which they summoned the day after the Battle of Newbury. (See *Clarendon's History*.) It is probable that the assailants who were defeated by the little garrison were ashamed of their failure and did not wish to make it public.—G.C.
[c] Added in another hand, probably that of the Earl of Manchester.

STATEMENT

BY

AN OPPONENT OF CROMWELL.

About the middle of December, now allmost two yeares sinc, the now Leiuctenant-Generall Cromwell being then captaine of a troope of horse under the command of the Earle of Essex, and I well knowinge that he had some part of his estate lyinge in the Ile of Ely, and a good part of my owne estate lying in the same Ile, and I well understood the dayly approch of the enimie upon our bordering counteys, and that the enimie and many of the inhabitants did plott to take that Ile for theire quarters, and soe to annoy all the adjacent counteys that bounde upon the sayd Ile.

Thes motives moved me to goe to Captaine Cromwell and to acquaint him with it, and did desire his assistance in that matter; he well conceived the danger and how it might be prevented, wherupon he moved the House to take it into their consideration; and he being in some hopes to attaine his desire he told me that he would not goe upon the buisness without I would take command and goe with him, which I could ill have done, I having soe much buisness both in the citye and country; yet I left all and raysed a troope of dragoones, horse, armes, bridles, saddles at my great charge, and payed my troope and officers for tenne weeks together out of my owne money by Captain Cromwell's perswasions, and many promises that I should have all my money with the first, which to this day I have never received one penny, though ther hath been great sums of money payd him, and he and some of his officers did, as I conceive, take away great sums of money from the subject injuriously and contrary to the ordinances of the Parliament.[a]

Now, to give an account of what I have observed and what I have heard and seene to doe this bleding state servis, here I shall declare Coll. Cromwell raysing of his regiment makes choyce of his officers, not such as weare souldiers or.men of estate, but such as were common men, pore and of meane parentage, onely he would give them the title of godly pretious men; yett his common practise was to casheire honest gentlemen and souldiers that ware stout in the cause as I conceive, witnes thos that did suffer in that case.

I have heard him oftentimes say that it must not be souldiers nor [the] Scots that must doe this worke, but it must be the godly to this purpose. When any new English man or some new upstart Independent did appeare ther must be a way mayd for them by casheiring others, some honest commander or other, and thos silly peopell putt in ther command. If you will examine this you will have proofe enough.

If you looke upon his owne regiment of horse see what a swarme ther is of thos that call themselves the godly; some of them profess they have sene vissions and had revellations.

Looke on Coll. Flettwoods regiment with his Major Harreson, what a cluster of preaching offecers and troopers ther is.

Looke what a company of troopers are thrust into other regiments by the head and shoulders, most of them Independents, whome they call Godly pretiouse men; nay, indeed, to say the truth, allmost all our horse be mayd of that faction.

If you looke on Coll. Russell's regiment, Coll. Mountegue's, Coll. Pickerin's, Coll. Rainsborough,[b] all of them proffessed Independents

[a] Originally written "peopell," and altered by another hand.
[b] An officer very much thought of by Cromwell. He was afterwards made an Admiral, but, being discarded by the navy, he returned to his command of foot, and was shortly after killed at Doncaster by a party from Pontefract who had intended to make him a prisoner.—G.C.

intire, and besides in most of our regements they have crammed in one company or other that they or ther offecers must be Independents. When will our warrs be ended by thos whose command gloryes in themselves whilst we have warr, and will be ther shame when we have peace?

The first winter after some buisness was done in Huntingdonshire, and the enemie had taken Crowland and fortified it; he then commanded me to Wisbidge, and there to maintaine guard upon the Crowlanders, which I did with mine owne troope onely, and att the springe took that towne in; yett that servisse, and all other done by me and others, must goe in his name or ells alls was not well. Collonel Cromwell, perceiving what might be done in the Ile by a smalle party, at my coming to him at Cambridge he told me he would make the Ile of Ely the strongest place in the world, and that he would out with all the wreches and ungodly men, and he would place in it godly and precious peopell, and he would make it a place for God to dwell in. I speaken to him to helpe me to some of moneys that I had layd out of my purse longe before and some moneys to pay my souldiers; he tolld me I might sett a tax upon the inhabitene of the Ile to pay myselfe, which I denyed, and thought it was not fitt for me to rayse moneys to pay myselfe.

About the seige of Linn Coll. Cromwell made Major Ireton deputy-governour of the Ile of Ely, who did report well of him, but he noe sonner came amounge us ther but he begins to levy great sums of money, some by ordinance of Parliament, some other wayes, pretending he would fortifie the Ile, and it is reported to me and others by the treasurer that he in aleuen mounths did receive at the least £15,000; yett at this day the Ile is in noe posture then it was in at the time when he came into it, onely it is become a meere Amsterdam, for in the chefest churches on the Sabbath day the souldiers have gonn up into the pulpitts both in the forenoone and the afternone and preached to the whole parish, and our ministers have satt in ther seatt in the church, and durst not attempt to preach, it being a common thinge to preach in private houses night and day, they having gott whole famalyes as Independents into that Ile from London and other places under ther command, lykwise haveing mayd poore men of that Ile captaines onely as I conceive because they proffess themselves Independents, and such as have filld dung carts both before they were captaines and since; they frequently rebaptise the peopell of that Ile, and thos captaines have power to commit to prison, and by a letter from Coll. Cromwell to the Committee, the coppy whereof I have, he doth command that Committey that they should not release any prisoner committed by his offecers, soe that the hole Ile is soe awde that they dare not seeke for ther libertyes.

I see at Ely upon the fial of letters to that Committee a letter from Collonell Cromwell to them that they should pay to his wife £5 per weeke towardes her extraordinaryes, which hath benn duly payd her a great while; I am sure there is noe ordinance of Parliament for that.

Major Ireton is still makeing a show of raysin of fortifications, but it is verely beleived it is but a pretene to gett moneys; covetuo[sness] doth best agree with a coward.

About a yeere since they ware very forward to drain that Ile, and I had some speeche with Collonell Cromwell here at London, I well knowing what ther aime was. The Coll. tolld me that he would draine it by the laboure of the souldiers, and Sir Cornelius Virmuden should doe it, and by draning he would fortifie it and make it invincible, and make a 100,000 ls. a yeare of thos grounds. I then asked the Collonell how the gentlemen that ware the undertakers should be satisfied for ther moneys layd out; he tolld me they did it for their owne ends and lett them loose ther moneys, and this should be for a publique good to settle godly men in. About that time Collonell Cromwell and Major Ireton ware seutours to the Committey at Cambridge for 3 score peices of ordinances for to strenghthen that Ile, and other vast demands they mayd to that Committe, as the Committe will satisfie you.

At our first being at Stamfourd after Crouland was taken ther was newes brought to Colonell Cromwell that ther was some lords of the King's side slaine, and he replyed that God fought against them, for God would have noe lording over his peopell, and he verily beleved that God would sweep away that lord in power out of this nation.

I did heare Collonell Cromwell about a yeare senc say to a gentleman as we ware going to the Earle of Manchester's quarters in St. Jones,[a] that if he had but Marsland and Holland joyned to the Ile of Ely he would make it the strongest thinge in the world, for ther he had three of the finest ports of the world, and that he could keepe them against all the strengh that could be mayd against them.

About some 4 dayes after there came two of Collonell Cromwell's troopers and an other man to them to my house in London and showed me a petition with a great many of hands and markes to it, and desired my hand to it, and I red the petition, and it was to the Parliament for libertye of consciens; I was troubled at it and tolld them I would have my hand cut of before I would sett my hand to it, and tolld them if any nation in the world ware in the ready way to Heaven it was the Scotts. They tolld me they thought I had been a godly man, but now they perceive what I was and went away; ever after Coll. Cromwell did sleight me.

At the springe, I being at Camebridge, we haveing ther intelligenc that Prince Rupert was comming to rayse our seige at Newark, I walkin over the market hill there with Collonell Cromwell, I speak to him thus: Sir, if you would march up to Newarke with but 1,500 of your horse you would spoyle Prince Rupert's market. He sayd againe ther is Sir John Meldrum and the rest would take the towne for all the Prince; I sayd to him againe it ware as cheape for our horse to march as to ly still in the stables; whereupon he was angry and bid me holld my tounge, I spoke I knew not what; yett he had then gallant horse, and I have heard him say that he had more horse in his troope that was at Edg hill then the Earle of Essex had in his whole armie.

[a] *Sic.*

When Collonell Cromwell this last summer quartered neare Ferrebrige, I was with him there, and I spake to him to quitt me from the armie; he gave me very good words, but delayed me till I came neare Yorke; but there Leuetenant-Collonell Whirly[a] tooke me by the hand and told me that if I would not be soe violent but resolve to agree with them he knew his Lieutenant-Generall would make me Collonell of ther regiment.

Shortly after I went to Wetherby to Collonell Cromwell to despath me, wher upon he told me if I had ben ruled by Major Ireton in the Ile then that all would have gon swetlye on, and the busn[ess] of the Ile had ben in a good forwardness, but yett if I would march with him, and be but conformable to pretious godly men, I should se that I should have better preferment then I did immagin; but I did desire to be gon and have my despatch; wher upon he writt to the Earle of Manchester to lett me have 3 mounths pay, my troop recruted with horse and armes, soe many as I marched withall from London, and to have the publique faith for the rest of my moneys and arreares. When we ware last at Huntington ther was the first report that the Earle of Essex was routed, and that he had totally lost his artillery and fought,[a] wherupon the Independents many of them ther did as it ware to show themselves soe joyfull[b] as though it had been a victory new gained to themselves. Ther is many a gentleman I believe had as sad a hart as my selfe that day will beare me wittnes of there rejoycing, the yett I doe beleive that if the state should protest against that sect, and they should have noe command, the best part of them would be noe Independents, for ther is many of them of ther opinion of ther preferment; but for the absolute Independent he is cruell without mercy, covetuoss without measure; he will have the spirrit though it be a false oune lying; is ther best guard, by which he defends

[a] Whalley.
[b] ? foot.—G.C.
[c] This amusing observation probably has much truth in it. The feeling between Presbyterians and Independents was, at this time, very bitter.—G.C.

himselfe and offends others, by takeing away the esteme of a man. Then his will is a law to doe what he will with him. This I can say by experience, the Lord of heaven deliver every honest man out of ther handes.

[Endorsed] delivered by Co.

CROMWELL'S NARRATIVE.

An accompt of the effect and substance of my narrative made to this House for soe much thereof as concernd the Earle of Manchester.

Being commanded by the House to give an accompt concerning the many opportunityes lost and advantages given to the enemy since the late conjunction of our armyes (ᵃ which seemed to be by some miscarriage or neglect in the conduct of the armyes), and especially of our not prosecuteing the victory at Newbery in time to prevent the King's rallying, of our suffering him (after he had recollected and gott to an heade againe) to relieve Dennington Castle and fetch off his ordnance (with all hee had left there ᵇ) in the face of our armyes, and to goe off without fighting; of our quiting of Newberry afterwards, and withdrawing the siege from Basing. I did in my narrative of the story freely declare that I thought the Earle of Manchester was most in fault for most of those miscarriages and the ill consequences of them. And because I had a greate deale of reason to think that his Lordshipp's miscarriage in these particulars was neither through accidents (which could not

ᵃ The marks of this parenthesis inserted by another hand.
ᵇ All the King's baggage waggons were left at Donnington Castle; also his papers (which his enemies would gladly have seized to turn to good account, as they did afterwards at Naseby). There was, besides, some treasure.—G.C.

be helped) nor through his improvidence only, but through his backwardness to all action, and had some reason to conceive that that backwardnes was not (meerely) from dulnes or indisposednes to engagement,[a] but (withall) from some principle of [b] unwillingnes in his Lordshipp to have this warre prosecuted unto a full victory, and a designe or [c] desire to have it ended by accommodacion (and that) on some such termes to which it might be disadvantageous to bring the King too lowe. To the ende therefore that (if it were soe) the state might not be further deceived in their expectations from theyr[d] Army, I did (in the faithfull discharge of my duty to the Parliament and kingdome) freely discover those my apprehensions, and what grounds I had for them, and, to that purpose,

1. I did not onely in the accompt of the particulars in question (since the conjunction of the armyes), but alsoe in many precedent[e] carriages upon former opportunityes since our coming, from Yorke (whereof I had been a wittnesse), declare his Lordshippes continued backwardnes to all action, his aversenes to engagement or what tendes thereto, his neglecting of opportunityes and declineing to take or pursue advantages upon the enemy, and this (in many particulars) contrary to advise given him, contrary to commaunds received, and when there had been noe impediment or other imployment for his army.

2. I did likewise declare how his Lordship had (both in words and actions) expressed much contempt and scorne of commaunds from the Parliament,[f] or the Committee of both kingdomes, which have required his advanceing westwards, and his desires and endeavour to have his army drawn back into his association to lye

---

[a] Originally written "fighting," but altered by another hand into "engagement."
[b] A word struck out here—perhaps "great."
[c] "a" has been struck out here.
[d] Altered from "the."
[e] Altered from, perhaps, "pretenced."
[f] This and many other similar passages look like an attempt to excite a prejudice against the accused.

idle there, while the businesse of the kingdome hath needed it, and the aforesaid commaunds required it to be employed elsewhere.

3. I did also declare in diverse circumstances of the said omissions and miscarriages what shuffleing pretences and evasions his Lordship had used, sometimes to delay and put off (till 'twas too late), sometimes to deny and avoyde things propounded to him, tending to action or engagement, when thadvantage and security of the same hath been clearely urged upon him, in which he had seemed studiously to decline the gayneing of such advantages upon the enemy, and sometimes to designe the draweing off the army off from the advantages it hath had, into a posture of lesse advantage.

4. I did alsoe declare some such speaches and expressions offred by his Lordship concurrent with the said series of his actions and carryages, whereby hee hath declared his dislike to the present warre, or the prosecution thereof, and his unwillingnesse to have it prosecuted unto a victory or ended by the sword, and desire to make up the same with some such a peace as himself best fancyed.

[Marginal notes in another hand.]

Of these heades the particulers of the first and third which I either toucht upon or related more at large in my narrative are briefely these:

The neglect of blocking up of Newarke.

That at our coming from Yorke (which was about the middle of July last) his Lordship having many advantages represented to him, and time enough to have taken or blockt up Newarke before he was comaunded into the south, and having then noe other employment or impediment to hinder his army from th'attempt thereof, did lye, first, with his whole army, eight or ten dayes about Doncaster, and afterwards with the greatest part of it about Lincolne for a month or more, without attempting anything either to reduce Newark or secure the country against it.

Tickhill Castle.

That lyeing at Doncaster, and Tickhill Castle being hard by, and Welbeck House with Sheffield and Bolsover Castle not farre off, he was very unwilling to the summoning of Tickhill Castle, and expressed much anger and threates against him that (being sent to quarter in the towne) did summon it, though upon the bare summons it was surrendered. And whereas, while he laye thereabouts, he might in that time have taken in those other garrisons alsoe, soe as to have had his army intire to march with him in good time against Newarke, hee would not be perswaded to send any party against any of them till he marcht from Doncaster, and then sending a party against Sheffeild, and afterwards (with much difficulty) giveing way for the same party in their returne to attempt Bolsover and Wingfield Mannor, hee made that serve for an excuse for that greater part of his army which went with him into Lincolneshyre to lye idle there, till the returne of the other, without attempting of any thing against Newarke, Belvoyr,ª Wereton, or Shelford. Newarke, Belvoyr, and other places neglected.

That in his way to Lincolne hee was very backward and hardly perswaded to march near Welbeck, to induce the surrender of that house.

That at Lincolne his Lordship being much prest by some of his officers to certaine proposicions for the takeing or blocking-up of Newarke, although the forces he had there with him all the while were sufficient for the service propounded, yet his Lordship first put off the consideration thereof till the returne of that party from Sheffeild, pretending that then hee would advise upon it.

But, when that party was returned, he further deferred the consideration of it, till, at last (through importunity), a councell being cald, his Lordship, labouring with various objections to avoyd the service, made the time left by those delayes a mayne argument against it. And when (notwithstanding all) the counsell did conclude, and his Lordship thereupon seemed to agree to drawe downe to quarter about Newarke, and doe what we would while we had time, yet his Lordship after this put it off againe with other pretences, and at last did nothing at all. Newarke still neglected.

That durcing the suspence of those propositions his Lordship, haveing letters from the Comittee soone after his coming to Lincolne to marche into Cheshire, was very angry and much displeased Letters to the Earl to send some horse to Cheshire.

ª Originally written " Bolsover."

thereat, sent up reasons against it, pretending a necessity of doeing something against Newarke to secure those partes before he would march soe farre thence, and in the answer thereto, being left to follow the service of those partes with his army, and required only to send some horse into Cheshire, hee was utterly against that alsoe, and (notwithstanding many letters out of Cheshire pressing him thereto, and signifying the great need and danger of those partes) yet he would not, nor ever offred to send any till after that resolution taken against Newarke as before, and then, though by later lettres thence he was advertised that their danger was past, and their need lesse then before, yet he pretended that he must needes send horse thither, and thereupon broke of the resolution against Newarke (that being soe putt off there went none).

That he caused his army (while it lay about Lincolne) to quarter upon our friendes in the more secured partes of the country, leaveing the other partes free for [a] the enemy to range on, rather then he would allow a sufficient part thereof to drawe downe towardes Newarke to quarter upon the enemy and to straiten and keep them in.

That though his Lordship while he thus lay idle about Lincolne (to avoyde the consideracons against Newarke) did sometimes pretend he would attempt the lesser garrisones about it (Belvoyre, Wereton, and Shelford), and was much desired thereto in case he would not meddle against Newarke, yet haveing put off the one, he did nothing against the other, not soe much as to secure the country against any of them.

Neglecting of Belvoyr, Wereton, and Shelford.

That by the said neglects thereof, while he had time, hee was occasioned for secureing of the country (when he was cald southward) to leave much the more force behinde out of his feild army, besides the force of the country, which otherwise by themselves [b] might have served to secure it, and the country soe cleared (as it might have been in that time) might have rayesed and maintayned

---

[a] " from " originally written.   [b] " by themselves " is an insertion.

a great accession of force [a] to our feild armyes; at which (with much more of the advantages of that service and disadvantage by the neglect) was timely and often foretold and urged to his Lordship by his officers while he lay idle as before, but his Lordship, from the time he came from Yorke (which was about July the fifteenth) till his coming from Lincolne (which was about September the third), did not vouchsafe to call his Councell of Warre to advise on any action or employment for his army, saveing that one Councell before mentioned upon the propositions against Newarke, when, indeed, the best opportunity and advantages for that service were lost by the former delayes. *The Earl came from York about July the 3rd (sic); from Lincoln towards the West, September 3rd.*

That though when (before any reall danger in the South appeared) these things were propounded for the cleareing and secureing of his Association, and that expressly to them his army might be the more free to leave those partes for the southerne service (if there should be need), his Lordshipp then (to avoyde these services) would sometimes pretend the keeping of his army free and ready to advance into the west if he should be required, yett when he sawe a reall danger and need of him in the West, being cald up and commaunded thitherwardes, hee was then much displeased thereat, and averse thereunto, pretending that he must provide for the security of his Association, that that was his proper business, and accordingly his Lo^p hath shewed himselfe both extreame backward to be drawne from his Association towards the West, and (being with much reluctance drawne but a little that way) he was averse to all good service thereaboutes, and desireing and endeavoring to be drawn back to his Assotiation agayne, as may appeare by what followes. *Unwillingness to march westwards.*

The first letters for his advance from Lincolne comeing about the end of August, hee made it September 13th ere his army got to St. Alban's, lyeing by the way about Peterborrough and Huntingdon fower nights or more, though he was in that time *13th September the army comes to St. Alban's.*

[a] "of force" is an insertion.

quickened by fresh letters and desired to hasten by his chiefe officers, whom he threatned to hang ᵃ for such advice.

The armyes stay at St. Alban's 8 or 9 dayes.
At St. Albanes he caused the army to lye still 8 or 9 dayes, and then marching slowly to Redding he stayd there till about October 16th, and then advanced not westwards directly ᵇ to Sir William Waller, but southwards to Basingstoke, notwithstanding a desire from this House, an Ordinance of both Houses, and many letters from the Committee of both Kingdomes, all requireing his speedy advance westward to Sir William Waller, and Sir William Waller's earnest desires in frequent letters to that purpose; there being this while nothing justly to hinder but that his army must have advanced directly to Sir William Waller, and the Lord Generall's and the City foot might soe have marched securely after them to have had the conjunction about Salisbury.

The Earl advanceth to Basing when commanded to march westwards, and desired by Sir W. W. letters.

This might have been securely done, the Earle of Manchester's foot with his owne and Sir William Waller's draggoones, being then above 6,000ⁿᵈ (without the Lord Generall's and the Citty regimentes), and the Kinges not soe many, and their horse with the Lord Generall's much superior to the King's. And, if his Lordship had advanced thither ᶜ accordingly, the King would not (in probability) have passed Salisbury river, or the plaines, for this winter; and soe the seiges of Dennington, Basing, and Banbury Castles had been secured and those places ours ere now, and the King by this time not had a foot on this side Salisbury, except Oxford, Winchester Castle,ᵈ and Wallingford, and those distressed by our quarters.

Advantages if the Earl had marched westward.

That by neglect hereof Sir William Waller being forced to give back to Andover and from thence to his Lordship, and the King coming on, his Lordship being then at Basingstoke, the City regiments then with him and the Lord-Generall's within seaven miles, and the King not come much nearer than Andover, his Lordship

The Earl's resolution to goe to Odiam but diswaded.

ᵃ ? Cromwell himself. See deposition before the Committee.—G.C.
ᵇ "directly" inserted afterwards.   ᶜ "thither" subsequently inserted.
ᵈ "Winchester Castle" subsequently inserted.

drew out his army in all haste to retreate to Odiam (leaving Basing and the besoigers exposed to the enemy)[a] had not Sir William Waller and Sir Arthur Haslerig, coming in the nicke, diswaded him from the dishonour of it.

That after this conjunction, wee being at Basing, neare 11,000 foote and about 8,000 horse and dragoones, and the King (with not above 10,000[d] horse and foote) marching by Kingscleare to Newberry, on Tuesday, October the 21th, it being agreed (as we thought) to march towards him or to interpose betwixt him and Redding about Aldermaston Heath, and our horse marching before to the Heath, our foot struck down to Swallowfield, and thence next day to Redding, as if we had declined to fight; and thus makeing fower days' march from Basingstoke to Newberry (which might have been little more than one th'other way), wee gave the King opportunity to have got cleare to Oxford (if hee would) without fighting, and stayinge there he had thereby[b] time to fortify himselfe against our approaches to Newberry, and by our coming that way wee gave him th'advantage of Dennington river interposed betwixt him and us, the passes whereof he soe comanded by the Castle and Dolman's house as put us to the hazard of divideing and the difficulty of marching about by Boxford to come upon him by Speene, which tooke two dayes more, whereas by a direct march from Basing, on the other side of Newberry river, we had had noe such interposicion betwixt us and Newberry, but the towne open and[c] naked to us, and neither the Castle nor the horse to annoy us (as they did) in our falling on ; and our horse being thus for these[d] six dayes, and two before, kept together out of quarter wayteing for that service (which the other way[e] might have been dispatcht in

The slownes of the march to Newberry and inconveniences attending it.

[a] The words in parenthesis subsequently inserted.
[b] "thereby" subsequently inserted.
[c] A deep river, the Keunett, however, flows through the town of Newberry, so that if some of the King's forces had possessed it the capture of the town would not have been easy.—G.C.
[d] "these" subsequently inserted.   [e] "the other way" subsequently inserted.

two dayes)ᵃ were both lessen'd and disabled for the service when they came to it, and from pursueing the victory when we had it.

That on Saturday, October 26,ᵇ when we came up to Redhill Feild, within shot of Shawe, and found the passes of the river ᶜ soe possest against us, it was agreed that the Lord General's and the City foote with the greatest parte of the horse should march about by Boxford and attempt to breake in upon the enemy on that side by Speene, and that his Lordship with his owne foote and about 1,500 horse should stay behind at Shawe side and fall on there at the same instant that he should perceive the other part to fall on at Speene (which was already in his viewe), yet that other part falling on upon Speene side about two o'clock next day, though he had notice of our engagement by the first fireing of cannon on both partes, and saw the enemy retreateing from hedge to hedge in disorder, and was much importuned to fall on by diverse about him (and his men likewise all the while within shott of Shawe), yet his Lordship would not suffer the men to fall on, but commanded the contrary, till allmost halfe an hour after sunsett,ᵈ about which time we on the other side (haveing gayned most of the hedges towardes Newberry Feild) did cease and drawe our men together to avoyd confusion in the darke by that scattred way of fighting; and his Lordship going on so late, his men presently fell fowle one upon another, and were put to assault Dolman'sᵉ house on that onely side where it was inaccessible (whereas 'twas open on the

Margin notes:
The Earl keepes not the agreement to fall on att Shawe when the other forces were engaged att Speene.

The Earl's men fall fowle one on the other in the darke; loose two peeces.

ᵃ "dayes" subsequently inserted.
ᵇ "Oct. 26" subsequently inserted.
ᶜ The Lamborn.—G.C.
ᵈ This differs, as far as I am aware, from the other accounts of the battle whether Royalist or Parliamentarian, which state that the Earl "fell on not later than 4 P.M." —G.C.
ᵉ Shaw House was protected by a broad rampart faced with stone (which now exists), a ha-ha, and a paling. The defence under Astley, Lisle, Page, and Thelwall, was desperate. The "open side" here spoken of seems to be that next Newberry, and would have necessitated a circuit of the house and an attack in rear of it.—G.C.

other), by which meanes he lost two peices of ordnance and many gallant men; whereas had he fallen on by daylight and according to agreement he might, on the open side, have taken that house with the men and ordnance in it, and, if so, we had betwixt our two bodyes in probability ruined the enemy, who had then had noe free passe over that river to gett away,[a] nor ground to stand on betwixt it and Newberry, nor comaunded by us.

That the enemy flying away in the night, his Lordship's body lying close by Dolman's house on that side of the river to which they fled, suffred them to pass over the river and goe by him[b] without prosecution; yea, suffred those in Dolman's house, which was on the same side of the river soe neare him, to goe cleare away with their owne and his ordnance.[c]

The Earl suffers those in Dolman's house to goe away.

The next morneing, being Munday, October 28th, all the horse on Speen side marching after the enemy, his Lordship with all the foot stay'd at Newberry, and the horse coming to Blewberry late that night, the enemy being got cleare over the river at Wallingford many houres before, and we haveing noe passe to follow them nearer than Abbinton, and our horse being tyred out with eight or nyne dayes continued hard duty without any quarters (as before), it was thought fit to let them goe to quarters that night, but something close together, and upon consultation it was judged both hazardous and uselesse to pursue further with the horse alone and intangle them amongst rivers and woodlands without foote; whereupon Sir William Waller, Sir Arthur Hasslerig, and myselfe (meeting by the way a letter from the Earle of Manchester to desire our return to Newberry) did goe back thither to get some foot to enable the horse for further pursuite. There we prest earnestly, first to have the whole army march speedily into the quarters

---

[a] "to gett away" subsequently inserted.

[b] "him" subsequently inserted.

[c] But Cromwell himself appears to have been equally to blame. The rest of the King's army went close past him with their own and captured orduance, which was also placed in safety at Donnington Castle.—G.C.

beyond Oxford (about Wittney, Burford, and Woodstock), where the enemy began to rally, and that being denied to have two or three thousand foot sent with the horse, but neither would be granted, his Lordship expressing extreame unwillingnesse thereto,[a] making excuses and delayes, speakeing for his returne into his Association, and much for peace; neither would he be perswaded to stirre till the Satturday following, November 2,[b] and then marching but to Harwell (eleaven miles towards Abbington) in two days (which at his returne hee dispatcht in one) he stopt there and would advance noe farther at all, some excuses being found, but especially unpassablenesse of the wayes to Abbington and beyond (though they were indeed good enough and proved both before and since to be passable for the enemy but not for us; and at this time, ere we went away, his Lordship allowed them passable to Abbington for the heavy carriage of his victuals, all which he sent thither); and the Lord Warreston and Mr. Crewe going from Harwell to London, possesst with that and other suggestions against advancing further and for our draweing back, his Lordship engaged himselfe by promise to them not to stirre thence till he received from them the directions of both Kingdomes, and made that promise[c] serve while hee stayed at Harwell to stop their mouthes that moved for advancing further.

And whereas (as it was timely represented to his Lordship) our timely marching into those quarters about Oxford and soe forward would have forced the enemy westward, prevented his re-collecting, occasioned his broken forces in frequent and hasty motions to droppe off[d] and dissipate still more, had hindred the conjunction with Rupartes and Garrett's forces, and kept the King from re-enforceing his army to appeare any more in the feild for this yeare. By our neglect thereof the King gathers the head againe with Rupartes and

The Earl refuseth to send foote to pursue the enemy.

Lord Wareston and Mr. Crewe.

Advantages of marching forward towards Oxon, et contra.

---

[a] "thereto" subsequently inserted.
[b] "Novemb. 2" subsequently inserted.
[c] Originally written "made this serve."
[d] "off" subsequently inserted.

Garrettes forces and otheres out of garrisones, gettes all to Oxford, and thence reinforceth his trayne and (the old being left at Denning-ton) resolves to fetch it thence and releive that place; and in order thereto ere we came from Harwell he drew thorowe Oxford, had a rendezvous or two at Bullington Green, yet drewe in againe, not dareing to come on that way till wee, draweing back to Newberry, gave him the way cleare by Dorchester and Wallingford, as followes.[a]

Wee being thus brought to the defensive part againe, while we lay [at] Harwell, some of us thought our present posture or some other thereabouts very good for lying in the Kinges way to fight ere he got over those plaines, and others propounded to crosse the rivers to Dorchester, to possess that towne and passe, and to quarter on this side the rivers, for more secure quarter and nearer interposition in the Kinges way to Dennington, and to prevent all other hazardes of his impressions towards London or other partes on this side Thames. All were against drawing back to Newberry that I know or heard save his Lordship onely. The inconveniencyes of that, and the greate advantages of the other postures, were represented to his Lordship. But those that were for any advance beyond Harwell his Lordship silenced with pretence of his promise not to remove till the directions came, yet the day before they came he did on Tuesday, November 5,[b] appoint a rendezvous for next morning at Compton, 4 or 5 miles back towards Newberry, without any counsell that I or those that were for the other postures know of, but (to stopp our mouthes) he pretended he would have a councell at the rendezvous[c] before he would resolve whether to dispose the army from thence, yet his Lordship goeing early to the rendezvous when we came thither we found the army ordred before to Newberry, in such haste as (I believe) the vanne was by noone

The Earl marcheth back to Newbury against advice.

[a] "as followes" subsequently inserted.
[b] "on Tuesday, Nov. 5," subsequently inserted.
[c] "at the rendezvous" subsequently inserted.

at or ^a neare Newberry, and this before any counsell met; his Lordship (when they were come ^b together) alleginge for what was done that he had there received the letteres from the Committee of both Kingdomes commanding his return to Newberry.

From this rendevous all the victualls (which were come up by water for the army) were sent by his Lordship to Abbington to excuse his not going beyond the river nor staying thereabouts to secure it. And that sending away of our victualls served afterwards for an occasion to necessitate the army to drawe homewards the sooner.

The drawing backe to Newberry caused the losse of Donington.

That our drawing back to Newberry was the chiefe or onely cause of our losse of the busines of Dennington, giveing the Kinge a cleare advantage to releive it, and putting us almost out of possibility to hinder him for haveing thus left the King the way clear by Dorchester to ^c Wallingford, and a large secure quarter in that corner on the north side of Thames close by his poste at Wallingford (beyond which we could not come to disturb or discover him, and by which he could come to annoy or discover us even to our quarters, and beate in small guards at pleasure). In that case if we at Newberry (upon every party appearing to drawe over at Wallingford and beate in our scowtes) should have drawn our horse together, the King might lye quiet with his body beyond the river till wee had been forced to dismisse them back to quarters weary and faint, and then might he have taken the opportunity to drawe speedily over, and be at the Castle before we could recall them, so as there was noe end of our draweing our horse together till certaine notice that the Kinges mayne ^d body was drawne over at Wallingford, and staying for that (since the notice would not come to us till three hours after or more) hee might, in that time, be

^a " by noone at or " inserted in place of " then."
^b " come " inserted.
^c " to " instead of " and."
^d " mayne " inserted.

got over the plaines, and consequently (before wee could possibly after that drawe our horse together or ᵃ get our foote out to interpose) he might be at the Castle and have donne his businesse.

And this being foretold and demonstrated before his Lordship upon the first intelligence of a party drawne out from Wallingford the day after we came to Newberry (which after drew in againe), and it being therefore moved to remove thence with our whole army to some better posture of interposition, his Lordship was content indeed to have had our horse drawne together if we would (which the King would soone have made us weary of as before), but would not hearken to drawe the foote thence till the King should come on, alledging that he might not quit Newberry; neither would he as yett ᵇ seeme to acknowledge but that (lying still till the King came on ᶜ) we might well enough prevent the releife of the Castle.

On the Fryday after, November 8,ᵈ the King draweing over in earnest, about two a clock advanced forward, and about five certayne ᵉ worde was brought us by a fugitive (sooner than we could otherwise expect). Wee sent orders immediately for our horse to meet att Redhill feild, but a counsell being called it was then found infeisible to drawe out time enough to interpose, and concluded that we must give the Castle for releived, and should only stand upon our guard till the enemy retreated, but then to fall on. And upon this the rendevous for the horse was altered to Newberry washe on the south side of the towne and river, the Castle and the enemy being on the north side. The next morneing (our horse being come together before day, and the King, contrary to expectation, staying all night at Ilsley, six miles short of the Castle) it was then urged by diverse that we might drawe out, but the debate being

ᵃ "or" inserted instead of "and."
ᵇ "as yett" a correction of the first writing.
ᶜ "there" as first written altered to "till the King came on."
ᵈ "Nov. 8" inserted.
ᵉ "certain" inserted.

held long till wee could not doe it time enough to interpose, the former resolution stood, his Lordship in these debates being most ready to finde the danger or infeisibility of draweing out to interpose, most earnest against it, and (in that last dispute) to protract time.

The enemy came on, releived the Castle, drew downe into Newberry feild, braved us at our workes, and (that while draweing their ordnance and carriages out of the Castle) in the evening they retreated up to the Castle and the heath beyond it. Upon intelligence that they continued their retreate in the night it was concluded that our horse should be drawne over into Shawe feild by three in the morning to pursue the enemy and endeavour to put them to a stand till our foote could come up, which were to follow by break of day. By light day we discovered the enemy not gone but drawne up on Winterbourne Heath,[a] and whereas before (while we thought they would be gone) we seemed forward to fight and regaine our lost honour, being now prest to hasten out the foote, there appeared much backwardnesse thereto, espetially in his Lordship (the foote with much importunity being nott got out[b] till about eleven a clock), and the enemy being not yet gone, soe as we might fight if we would and have the advantage (before pretended to be lookt for) of a retreating enemy. His Lordship having now noe further evasion left to shift it off under another name, playnely declared himself against fighting, and haveing spent much time in vieweing the enemy while they drewe off, and preparatory discourses, a councell being call'd, hee made it the question whether 'twere prudent to fight. With all earnestnesse and sollicitousnesse he urged all discouragements against it, opposed all that was said for it, and, amongst other things, it being urged that if now we let the King

[a] About two miles from Donnington Castle in a northerly direction. I have somewhere read that the King halted here for Divine Service, this being Sunday, 10th November.—G.C.

[b] "not got out" an alteration.

goe off with such honour it would give him reputacion both at home and abroade to drawe assistance to him, especially from France, where (wee heard) endeavours were to get ayde for him. But, if wee beate him now, it would loose him every where, and therefore it concern'd us now to attempt it before such ayde came. His Lordship replyeing told the councell he would assure them there was noe such thing, adding (with vehemence) this principle against fighting : that if we beate the King 99 times he would be King still, and his posterity, and we subjects still ; but if he beate us but once we should be hang'd, and our posterity be undonne. Thus 'twas concluded not to fight, the King suffred to march off unsought (being within a mile of us), and we retreated into Newberry.

The King (thus encouraged) retires not back towards Oxford, but goes to Marleborough, hovers there for an opportunity to releive Basing alsoe. The Earle of Manchester (the while)[a] hangs homewardes to be gone into his Association his agentes, and savour (some) to procure command for it, (others) to stirre up the soldieres mindes to it, for both extremityes are needlessly put upon the soldieres, and pretended to be greate where they are not; his Lordship's treasurer telling the soldiers (when they complayn'd of their wantes) that they should have neither money nor clothes till they came into the Assotiation, but then they should have both.

And whereas (for our coming back to Newberry from Harwell)[b] 'twas sometimes pretended by his Lordship that Newberry must be fortifyed for a winter quarter, yet when we came there noe [c] order was taken for it, and though the importance of that place (espetially in reference to the seige of Basing) was by the former councell

---

[a] " (the while) " inserted.
[b] " from Harwell " inserted.
[c] Clarendon says, " that after the failure of the last assault on Donnington Castle the commanders could not agree about anything, but remained at Newberry quarrelling amongst themselves.—G.C.

judged to be greate, and 'twas readily apprehended by his Lordship as a reason to avoide our marching out to fight the King, least he should wheele about into Newberry and soe releive Basing, yet afterwards (the King staying at Marlebrough for an opportunity to releive Basing) the Earle of Manchester was very forward to quitt Newberry, and at last, upon intelligence of a greate party drawne out from Marleborowe to goe to Basing another way, wee did drawe out from Newberry; but then it was pretended to the councell that we should goe to Kingscleare for a more direct interposicion in the King's way to Basing, and that there we might fight with him upon the downes, if he came that way, and lye ready (if he should bend towardes Newberry) to repossesse it before him; and on those grounds onely and to that end was our remove agreed to in a full councell. But being thus got out, and upon our way to Kingscleare, having intelligence that the King was coming on [a] by Hungerford towardes Newberry, his Lordship would then neither go on to Kingscleare nor return into Newberry, but upon new pretences (without the councell of warre) turn'd his course to Aldermarston (which was five miles homewards from Newberry, and seaven miles nearer home then Kingscleare.) And, though Kingscleare was the knowne direct roade to Basing, yet he pretended to turn to Aldermarston with intent to goe directly to Basing, and that he would fight the King there which way soever he should come if he attempted to releive it. This gave some satisfaction for present, but from Aldermarston his Lordship would not be got to Basing (makeing excuses);[b] but with much adoe being got out next day to Mortimer heath, he would not be perswaded to goe on any further, alledging that many of his soldiers were run to Redding, and more would goe thither (being got so neare it); that (when he pretended for Basing) draweing the army to Aldermarston (which was cleare out of the way) he brought the soldiers

---

[a] "on " inserted.
[b] " excuses " an alteration ; originally written " promises."

soe neare Redding that they would be running thither, and then made their running thither an occasion to avoyde going to Basing at all, and at last to drawe all to Redding.[a]

[Indorsed] Lieutenant-Generall Cromwell's Narrative.[b]

---

[a] The words "and withdrewe the seige from Basing," with which the paper concluded, have been struck out.

[b] This narrative may or may not correspond exactly with the charge of Cromwell in the House. Probably it differs in many particulars. It is quite unlike the usual style of Cromwell. This document is compiled with great care and skill, and is remarkable for terseness and perspicuity; and is also notable for the absence of scriptural language and allusions common to most of Cromwell's speeches and letters. It may be the work of several hands. Probably Waller and Hasilrigg had something to do with it. A question might arise as to whether Vane, who was no doubt very active in the "Independent Plot," may not have had a chief hand in its compilation. It is to be regretted that there appears to be no answer on the part of the Earl of Manchester extant. It does not, however, appear by any means certain that the Earl of Manchester was ever permitted to see this particular document. It is worthy of note that no allusion is made to the failure of the attempt to take Donnington Castle by assault as described by Clarendon.—(Clar. Hist. vol. iv. p. 589, *et seq.*)

NOTES OF EVIDENCE

AGAINST

THE EARL OF MANCHESTER.

1. That the Earl by his constant backwordnesse to action, and unwillingnesse to ingage with the enimys, hath lost many faire advantages and opportunityes, and hath neclected the commands of Parlement and booth Kindomes in matters of importance.

? Harrison. 1. Ha. that ther weare propositions made to the Earl when he came from Yorke to beleauger Newarke, which was a thing very feasable, but the Earl wold not consent unto it.

? Rich. 2. Ri. that after the Earle came from Yorke he found him allwayes backward to putt his armye to action.

? Walton or Watson. 3. Wa. that when ther wear propositions made to the Earl to putt his army into action he was very backward, and, beeing advised to build a fort a[t] Musham Bridge to block upp Newark, he refused it, and when ther wear propositions sent to march into Cheshire he refused to goe.

? Jones. 4. Jn. that when the Earl had advantages to blocke up Newarke he shewed himselfe very backward, and lay still at Pomfrett, Doncaster, and Lincolne, about 9 weekes, contrarye to the advice of his counsill of warr.

☞ Then wear ther 16 letters reade from the Committee of booth Kindomes.

14th and 28th August to Lincoln.
14th October to Reading.
2nd Sept. 9, 11, 26, 28 Sept.
And others to Newberye.

☞ Then wear the orders of the House of Parlement to the Earle reade.

5. Hen. Ha. that the Earle refused to martch from Lincolne to the west, and sayd that yf any moved he shold goe westward he wold hange him, and venture himselfe to be casherred rather then he wolde goe.

6. Cr. when he desired the Earl to goe westward he sayd he wold hang him or them that shold move it. ? Cromwell

☞ Then was an order of the House, made 8th October, read, requiring his remove from Reding to Shaftesburye, yett he did not then martch untill the 10th of October, and when he did he went to Basing Stocke and not westward as he was ordered.

7. Jr. That the Earl went to Basing when he shold have gone to Salisburye to have mett Sir William Waller.

8. S. W. W. that it was his opinion that my Lord George and the Earl might have joyned with him at Shaftsbury, which yf it had binn doone the enimye could not have releived Dunnington, but the seidge wold have continued still. ? SirW.Waller.

9. Sir A. He. that ther weare severall letters sent to the Earl to goe to Sir W. W., which not being observed, Sir W. W. was constrayned to retreat, and by that the enimye advanced. ? Hesilrigg.

10. Ha: that the Earl retreated to Odium out of the way, and at that time he had 7,000 foote and 7,000 horse, which was a sufficient force then to have fought the King's whole army.

The principall backwardness of the Earl appeered at Shawsfeild or Speein, neere Xuberye, wherby agreement the Earl was to fall on presently after the warning peece was shott off, but that he did not doe untill an hour and a halfe after it was shott off.

1. Rawlins: he was present, and did presse the Earl after the warning was given to fall on, and heare Watson come and tell him that the warning pece was shott off.

2. Wat: that the Earl did not fall on untill a quarter of an hower after sunn sett, two howers after the fight begun at Speen, and after the warning, &c. ? Watson.

3. Coll. Hooper agrees it was a quarter after sunn sett.
    Wever.

• 4. Col. Norton agrees, and that the Earle was verye backward to prosecute the victorye after the battayle.

5. Col. Jones: that fower dayes after the batayle he told the Earle that he had a great opportunitye to make an end of the warre, to which the Earle replyed that he had reason now to return to his Association and refresh his men.

6. Coll. Hooper: that he advised the Earle to send out scouts for discoverye how, wher, and in what condition the enimye was inn, and did relate to the Earl the great good he shold have done yf he had prosecuted the victorye.

7. Sir W. W.: that after the baytale he did pursue the enimye, but was sent for back once or twice by the said Earl, but he refused to come.

8. Sir A. He: that they pursued the enimye as farr as Blewberrye, but wear sent for back; yf they had not they had kept the enimye from ever joyning; that the Earl wold not advance, but yf he had advanced from Spine it had binn of great advantage.

The meanes by which Dennington came to be relieved was by the Earl default.

? Harrison. 1. Ha: If the Earl had continued betwin Wallingford and Newberry as he was advised to doe, he had kept the castle from beeing releived.

2. Harrington }
3. Ireton } agree in this.

4. Wat: that he hath binn at many counsills of warr and he never heard the Earl give his advise for fighting or advancing.

? Pickering. 5. Pic: that the Earl was allwayes backeward to ingage himselfe.

6. Ri: that the Earl since he came from Yorke was allwayes backword in the service.

---

and therfore it is good reason to conceive that the Earl's backwordnesse was out of designe to protract the warr.

1. Proved by his actions as formerlye.
2. By words as followethe.
　1. Ir: that he heard the Earl say that this warr wold never be ended by the sword but by accommodation, and that he wold not have it ended by the sword, and that yf we should beat the King 99 times and he beat us but once we shold all be hanged.
　2. Wall: agrees in the same.
　3. Collonell Jones: he heard the Earl say "God send us peace; for God will never prosper the victorys to us soe as to make them cleer victoryes to us."
　4. Ha: he heard the Earl say that this warr wold never be ended by fighting.
　5. Ir: at Huntingdon the Earl did receive the commands from ? Ireton. the Comitte of Kindomes and Parlement with much indignation, and sayd they were ridiculous and frivilous, and he must not looke for reason in their commands.
　6. Cr: that he would hang him or them that shold move him to ? Cromwell. goe to the west, and one of my Lord's friends in the Earl's presence sayd that the Parlement could not rule in an army which the Earl rebuked not.
　7. Desb: the Earl say that yf the Comitte of the Assossiation ? Desborough. shold move him to come to them he wold doe it all tho were hanged for it.
　8. Wat: that his army was raysed by the Assossiation, and could not be removed without ther consents, and the Earl sayd that yf he shold be commanded awaye without ther consent he wold be hanged or cashered before he wold obey.
　9. Pic: the Earl sayd that the Parlement never cared how they hurried ther forces soe they satisfied them that desired it.[a]

[a] This document appears to be a summary of the evidence given (in support of Cromwell's charge) before the Committee of which Tate was chairman. The witnesses appear to be mostly either connections or partizans of Cromwell.—G.C.

INDEX.

Abingdon, troops ordered to march to, 17, 18
Ayloff, Colonel, ordered to reinforce Manchester, 15

Basing, the siege of, to be raised by Walker, 17; orders to Manchester to raise the siege of, 47
Behre, Commissary-General, marches towards Somerton and Weymouth, 26

Charles I. expected to go to Oxford, 26; expected to march by Newbury and Abingdon, 35; reported to be marching eastwards, 42; said to be about Blandford, 43; fights the Battle of Newbury, 50; goes to Wallingford, 54; comes to the succour of Donnington Castle, 56; relieves the castle, 57
Cheshire invaded by Prince Rupert, 3
Chester, Rupert's strong position at, 9
Clavering, Colonel, with Prince Rupert, 3
Cleveland, the Earl of, taken prisoner, 50
Crawford, Major-General, sent to Sheffield, 6; arrests Packer, 59; his ruin said to have been intended by Cromwell, 62
Cromwell, Lieutenant-General, his horse regiment at Banbury, 29; is left near Oxford, 33; ordered to join Manchester, 43; joins Manchester, 45; is present at the Battle of Newbury, 57; complains of Packer's arrest, 59; supports a petition to Manchester, 60; accused of setting a robber at liberty, 61; his proceedings criticised, 62-70; his selection of Independent officers blamed, 71; his proposals for defending the Isle of Ely, 74; petition of his troopers for liberty of conscience, 75; defends his proceedings, 78
Cuttenburg, Mr., sent to view Reading, 33

Donnington Castle reconnoitred by Manchester, 32; the King's forces drawn up near, 49; attack upon ordered, 52; succoured by the King's forces, 55
Dorrington, Sir Francis, about to join Manchester, 17

Ely, Isle of, proceedings of Ireton in the, 73
Essex, recruits from, not to be taken by Manchester, 8, 13

Fairfax, Sir Thomas, left by Manchester at York, 1
Fleetwood, Colonel, ordered to place himself at Cromwell's disposal, 30; recalled by Manchester, 34

Gerard, Sir Charles, leaves Wales, 17
Glemham, Sir Thomas, his march reported by Manchester, 30

Hammond, Colonel, loses some guns, 65

Independents supported by Cromwell, 61; selected as officers by Cromwell, 71; are said to be pleased by the news of Essex's defeat, 76
Ireton, Major, Deputy-Governor of the Isle of Ely, 73

Ludlow, Colonel, ordered to Wiltshire, 53

Manchester, Earl of, separates from the Scotch army, 1; takes Tickhill Castle, 2; determines to march southwards, 3; complains of want of money, 4; receives the surrender of Welbeck, 6; recruits for, 8; hesitates to besiege Chester, 9; recommends the siege of four castles, 10; thinks he ought to obtain recruits from Essex, 13; ordered to send forces to

CAMD. SOC. P

Cheshire and Abingdon, 14; ordered to send troops against Prince Rupert, 19; directed to march towards Woodstock, 20; marches southwards, 24; directed to march to Abingdon, 26; stopped by the breaking of the bridge at Maidenhead, 28; remains at Reading, 31; reconnoitres Donington Castle, 32; sends orders to Fleetwood, 34; reports the disposition of his troops, 36; reports that the King is advancing 41; is ordered to send for Cromwell, 42; collects his forces, 43-48; comes in sight of the enemy near Newbury, 48; fights a battle at Newbury, 50; ordered to attack Donnington Castle, 52; refrains from attacking the King, 55; danger of mutiny in his army, 61; his proceedings before and at the Battle of Newbury criticised, 62-70; his proceedings criticised by Cromwell, 78; Notes of Evidence against, 96

Middleton, Lieut.-Colonel, marches towards Somerton and Weymouth, 26

Montagne, Colonel, his regiment refuses obedience to Crawford, 61

Montrose, Earl of, with Prince Rupert, 8

Newbury, Battle of, 50, 66

Newcastle, intention of the Scots upon, 3

Newcastle, Marquis of, his family taken at Welbeck, 6

Norwich, Sir John, to be cashiered if he does not obey orders, 21

Packer, Lieutenant, disobeys Crawford, 59

Pickering, Colonel, his regiment refuses obedience to Crawford, 61

Rich, Lieutenant-Colonel, sent by Cromwell to Crawford, 59

Rupert, Prince, marches into Cheshire, 3; threatens Newark, 4; his strong position at Chester, 9; marches southward, 18; goes towards Bristol, 22, 23; arrives at Wells, 32

Scotch Army, the, quarters at Leeds and Wakefield, 1; aims at taking Newcastle, 3

Sheffield, spoil done by the garrison, 5; capture of, 15

Throgmorton, Sir Baynham, marches from Wales, 17

Tickhill Castle surrenders to Manchester, 2

Waller, Sir William, leaves Abingdon, 17; ordered to stay about Shaftesbury, 30; joins Manchester, 47

Wallingford, the King at, 54

Welbeck surrenders to Manchester, 6

Wingfield Manor, surrender of, 16

www.ingramcontent.com/pod-product-compliance
Lightning Source LLC
Chambersburg PA
CBHW020915230426
43666CB00008B/1464